THE W-FILES

True Reports of Wisconsin's Unexplained Phenomena

by jay rath

Trails Books
Madison, Wisconsin

Library of Congress Catalog Card Number: 97-61553
ISBN: 0-915024-59-4

Editor: Elizabeth McBride
Designer: Kathie Campbell
Illustrations: Jay Rath

Printed in the United States of America by Master Litho.

06 05 04 03 02 01 00   6 5 4 3

This book was not approved, prepared, licensed or endorsed
by any entity involved in creating or producing "The X-Files."

Trails Media Group, Inc.
P.O. Box 5650
Madison, WI 53705
(800) 236-8088
email: info@wistrails.com
www.trailsbooks.com

For my good friend, George.

TABLE OF CONTENTS

ACKNOWLEDGMENTS

The material in this book comes from a variety of sources, including personal interviews, conversations with other researchers, books, newsletters, newspaper archives and the collections of the State Historical Society of Wisconsin.

I am especially indebted to Loren Coleman, one of America's leading investigators of unexplained phenomena, who generously allowed me to quote from his work and who provided the photo of the "kangaroo." Frank Joseph similarly allowed me to use material from his books, *The Lost Pyramids of Rock Lake* and *Atlantis in Wisconsin*. Readers are advised to seek out the works of both these gracious writers. Mr. Joseph's books are available from Galde Press, P.O. Box 65611, St. Paul, MN 55165.

Jennifer Cook-Jindrich was my eyes and ears in Eagle River. In Elmwood, Joanne Baier selected the best UFO sightings and generously made available materials collected by the public library there. Thanks also to Cindy Becker and Shelly Schmidt for helping me on my Elmwood field trip. But for my friend George, this book would more properly be dedicated to Molly Spillman, who provided essential moral support and put up with my moods.

A number of people helped in the production of the electronic manuscript. They include: Mary Bergin, Suzanne Boben, Samara Kalk, Del and Sara Lamont, Ann Burt-Meyer and—most especially—John Najem.

INTRODUCTION

As we near the millennium, why should a collection of a state's unusual phenomena be of interest?

First of all, everyone likes a good story, and mysterious tales, especially local ones about UFOs, Bigfoot and the like, are especially interesting. It's exciting to think that a flying disc landed and disgorged alien robots. It's more exciting to think (know?) that it happened in our town or the next county over. As it happens, Wisconsin has an extra-large helping of unexplained phenomena, and I'm not the only one who thinks so. The CIA does, too. More on that later.

But, in addition to their possible scientific and entertainment merits, stories of unusual phenomena are valuable for what they tell us about ourselves. This line of thought crystallized for me in a discussion with Professor Robert A. Brightman, professor of anthropology at the University of Wisconsin-Madison. That was in 1984, when I first started writing about unexplained phenomena.

Brightman is a little different from the typical anthropologist; he investigates Bigfoot sightings. Now, anthropology covers several disciplines, including studies of manlike animals of prehistory; it's a natural field for anyone interested in Bigfoot sightings, and in fact several university researchers believe that some Eastern European reports of the Bigfoot monster may describe a tribe of relict hominids, Neanderthal. But anthropology also covers human culture of the moment. This is Brightman's area of interest. He doesn't study Bigfoot reports because he wants to prove whether or not the creature exists. In fact, he believes it does not. His interest is in why people want to believe the stories about Bigfoot. Brightman doesn't scrutinize Bigfoot. He scrutinizes us.

"Images like Bigfoot—images between humans and animals—seem to be common to people of all states of society," Brightman told me in '84. "If it's not universal, it's close to universal."

As Brightman and history show, there have long been tales of half-human, half-animal monsters, such as the centaur, the minotaur and the mermaid. Today, there is Nepal's Yeti, or Abominable Snowman. In Russia, they call a similar creature Omah. In China, it is the Wildman. On our continent the Yeti is termed Bigfoot or, depending on the region, Sasquatch, Bushman, Creek Devil, Big Mo, Smy-a-Likh, Mountain Devil or Dsonqua. Wisconsin's Indians called this creature Windigo. And new creatures are always springing up. Very recently, Puerto Rico has been plagued by the Chupacabras, a sort of vampiristic gremlin with talons. It was unknown two years ago. Puerto Rico enjoyed a brief "Chupas" monopoly, but now it seems that the rest of the world must have one, too. Today, the Chupas is sighted as far away as Japan and as near as Florida and maybe, as I'll show, in Wisconsin as well.

What purpose do these monsters serve? Brightman talks of a psychological need to distinguish human culture from nature—in other words, to know how we are different. As an example, let's look at the three different kinds of Bigfoot reports.

First, there is Bigfoot the Monster: Under this heading fall the stories of a huge, slavering creature that stalks humans and attempts to kill and eat them. This Bigfoot is in the classical tradition of the wild man and werewolf.

Second, there is Bigfoot the House Pet: a docile, dependent creature in need of human aid. (An example of this would be the story of an Alberta, Canada, farm girl who discovered a female Sasquatch in the family barn. The poor thing—the monster, not the girl—was stricken and in labor! The girl assisted in the delivery, plucky lass. In the dawn, the creature left, but not before it expressed its heartfelt gratitude in a touching, hypnotic gaze.)

Third, there is Bigfoot, Friend of Man. In this category, injured hunters and travelers are befriended by the gentle giants, who aid them. Sometimes the creatures, who can speak, lead the humans to a cave or dwelling where Big Nuclear Foot Families are observed, complete with teenagers.

In all of these stories, human qualities are contrasted with those of a beast, an animal we call Bigfoot. Bigfoot is wild; we are civilized. Bigfoot is helpless; we are skilled. Bigfoot is subservient; we are dominant. The stories define the rules for membership in the human club: We are not animals, we are not monsters—we are not Bigfoot.

That's sort of a desperate cry, isn't it? And it's just one of many.

Some unexplained phenomena, real or not, seem to serve emotional, as well as psychological, needs. It is interesting to note, for example, that although strange objects have been seen in the skies since Biblical times, it has only been since 1947 that UFOs were thought to be spacecraft. Before that, they were "mystery airships," perhaps dirigibles. Even earlier, UFOs were attributed to God. Consider Ezekiel's Wheel in the Old Testament. The story has become a cliched opening to UFO books, but for the uninitiated, here it is. Wrote the prophet: "In the 30th year, in the fourth month, on the fifth day of that month [it already reads like an Air Force UFO report], as I was among the exiles by the river Chebar, the heavens were opened, and I saw visions of God." Ezekiel beheld a stormy wind and a great cloud, "with brightness round about it, and fire flashing forth continually, and in the midst of the fire, as it were gleaming bronze." From this whatever-it-was came "the likenesses of four living creatures" that also "sparkled like burnished bronze." The creatures each took smaller craft that gleamed like chrysolite, a greenish-yellow gem, "their construction as it were a wheel within a wheel." To Ezekiel, this was God, or at least godly.

Centuries later, we began to depend less on religion and more on science to explain the wonders around us, and the "wheel within a wheel" became a spacecraft. After World War II and the invention of the atom bomb, people began to fear that science might rule us, instead of the other way around. When flying saucers were "discovered" just two years after the war, in 1947, it was pleasant to believe that a more advanced society was out there. That meant we had not yet reached the apogee of civilization. We, too, could advance and flourish. Perhaps such futuristic visitors would have warnings and messages of peace for us. Maybe they'd even keep a friendly eye on us and our bombs, the way you'd watch the neighbor boy if he started fooling with a shotgun on the front porch. Perhaps the first meetings with the alleged aliens revealed that they were on just such a mission.

Today, there is as much reason to believe that UFOs and their occupants are from God as to believe they are spacecraft. As the century closes, the aliens have turned nasty, abducting us and doing reproductive experiments. New Age philosophies first put forth in the 1950s continue to spark new theories about the visitors' origins: They are angels; they are ourselves traveling from the future; they are beings from a parallel universe; they are ourselves from a future parallel universe, only perceived as angels—a higher state of being that we are just beginning to comprehend. And they are here to help us reach that nobler plane. Or sterilize and conquer us. Take your pick.

I'm not convinced they aren't Martians or Moon Men, but I'll allow as how stories of unexplained phenomena may help us better understand the human condition.

I did not, however, investigate these events in service to that worthy philosophy.

I did it because it was fun.

An Invitation

If you have stories about unexplained phenomena in Wisconsin, Iowa, Minnesota, Michigan or Illinois, please share them with me. I can be reached in care of Wisconsin Trails, P.O. Box 5650, Madison, WI 53705.

Selected Bibliography

Ileaned hard on a number of sources, especially archives at the State Historical Society of Wisconsin, notably the very rare brochures collection of Charles Brown. To that open-minded jazz-age historian, everyone interested in Wisconsin folklore owes a great debt.

Many newspaper morgues offered up their evidence, especially that of the *Capital Times* in Madison, and also that of the *Eau Claire Leader Telegram*. Other printed works include:

Blum, Howard. *Out There*. New York: Simon and Schuster, 1990.

Coleman, Loren. *Mysterious America*. Boston: Faber and Faber, 1983.

Corliss, William. *Handbook of Unusual Natural Phenomena*. Garden City, New York: Anchor Press/Doubleday, 1983.

Ebon, Martin. *Atlantis: The New Evidence*. New York: New American Library, 1977.

Fawcett, Lawrence, and Barry Greenwood. *Clear Intent: The Government Coverup of the UFO Experience*. Englewood Cliffs, N.J.: Prentice-Hall Inc., 1981.

Fowler, Raymond. *Casebook of a UFO Investigator*. Englewood Cliffs, N.J.: Prentice-Hall, Inc., 1981.

Green, John. *The Sasquatch File*. Agassiz, British Columbia: Cheam Publishing Ltd., 1973.

Hall, Richard, ed. *The UFO Evidence*. Washington, D.C.: National Investigations Committee on Aerial Phenomena (NICAP), 1964.

Joseph, Frank. *Atlantis in Wisconsin*. St. Paul: Galde Press, 1995.

_____. *The Lost Pyramids of Rock Lake*. St. Paul: Galde Press, 1992.

Landsberg, Alan. *In Search of ...*. New York: Everest House, 1978.

Mallan, Lloyd. *The Official Guide to UFOs*. New York: Science and Mechanics Publishing Co., 1967.

Napier, John. *Bigfoot*. New York: Berkley Medallion Books, 1972.

Olsen, Thomas, ed. *The Reference for Outstanding UFO Reports*. Riderwood, Maryland: UFO Information Retrieval Center Inc., 1966.

Scully, Frank. *Behind the Flying Saucers*. New York: Henry Holt and Company, 1950.

PANCAKES FROM SPACE!

*"I have decided that when
150 million persons are rated crazy
it's the psychiatrist who is cracked."*

Frank Scully*

Wisconsin's strangest close encounter of the third kind must surely be the incident during which Joe Simonton was given three pancakes by "Italian-looking" aliens.

A close encounter of the third kind is an actual meeting between humans and extraterrestrials, and Simonton's is easily the state's best-known. Despite the unlikely manner in which the story unfolded, the episode survived a rigorous assessment by the U.S. Air Force and is carried in their files as "unexplained."

In 1961, Joe Simonton was a plumber, auctioneer and Santa Claus —annually, for the Eagle River Chamber of Commerce. He reported his age as 55 or 60, depending on the interviewer. At 11 a.m., April 18, Simonton was having a late breakfast when he heard a sound like that of a jet being throttled back, something like the sound of "knobby tires on wet pavement." He went into the yard and saw a flying saucer drop out of the sky and hover over his farm. It was silver and "brighter than

---

* Yes, pioneer UFO researcher Frank Scully is the person who has given his name to one of the characters on the television program, "The X-Files." Scully's 1950 book, *Behind the Flying Saucers*, has been much maligned, and he is all but ignored by current researchers. However, Scully's analysis of the field in general set the agenda for almost all areas of investigation that followed.

chrome," 12 feet in height and 30 feet in diameter. On one edge were what appeared to be exhaust pipes, 6 or 7 inches in diameter.

The disc landed and a hatch opened. Inside were three dark-skinned aliens, each about 5 feet tall and weighing about 125 pounds. They appeared to be between 25 and 30 years old and were dressed in dark blue or black knit uniforms with turtleneck tops, and helmetlike caps. They were clean-shaven, Simonton said, and "Italian-looking."

The aliens did not speak in his presence, but they had a silvery jug with two handles, heavier than aluminum but lighter than steel, about a foot high. It seemed to be made out of the same material as the craft. Simonton said it was "a beautiful thing, a Thermos juglike bottle quite unlike any jug I have ever seen here [on Earth]."

Through ESP or something, Simonton got the idea that the aliens wanted water. He left the visitors, filled the jug from the water pump in his basement, then returned to the craft and gave the jug back. To do this, he had to brace himself against the UFO's hull and stretch up. From the subsequent Air Force report: "Looking into the [saucer] he saw a man 'cooking' on some kind of flameless cooking appliance." The alien was preparing pancakes.

The interior of the UFO was dull black, even the three "extremely beautiful" instrument panels, and had the appearance of wrought iron. The contrast between the dark interior and shiny exterior so fascinated Simonton that he later said that he "would love to have a room painted in the same way."

In return for the water, one of the aliens—the only one with narrow red trim on his trousers—presented Simonton with three of the pancakes, hot from the griddle. As he did so, the alien touched his own forehead, apparently a salute in thanks to Simonton for his help. Simonton saluted back. Each of the pancakes was roughly 3 inches in diameter and perforated with small holes.

The head alien then connected a line or belt to a hook in his clothing and the hatch closed. The saucer rose about 20 feet and took off to the south, at a 45-degree angle. Its wake left a blast of air that tossed the tops of nearby pine trees. The craft took only two seconds to disappear from view.

Simonton ate one of the pancakes, ostensibly in the interest of science. "It tasted like cardboard," he told the Associated Press. The other two pancakes he gave to Vilas County Judge Frank Carter, a local UFO enthusiast. Carter, who called the aliens "saucernauts" (I prefer

"Italiens"), said he believed Simonton's story since he could not think of any way in which the farmer might profit from a hoax. Carter's son, Colyn, today a lawyer in Eagle River, told me, "I recall as a youngster that my dad took it very seriously."

Judge Carter sent the pancakes to what was then the country's top investigative group, the National Investigations Committee on Aerial Phenomena (NICAP). They refused the opportunity to check it out. That put a damper on Judge Carter's plans; he had wanted to hold a seminar on the incident.

By this time, Simonton said, he was "irked by reporters making fun of the situation and laughing."

UFO activity, however, continued in the area. Four days after Simonton's experience, on April 22, Sarvino Borgo, an Eagle River insurance agent, was driving on Highway 70 when he saw a UFO. It was about a mile away, he estimated, four miles west of town and in the general vicinity of the farm where Joe Simonton lived. The next day a report came in from nearby Rhinelander. The sheriff's office there stated that it had been contacted by two youths who said that they, their mother and their sister had seen a UFO.

In response to all this, the Air Force dispatched its civilian UFO investigator, J. Allen Hynek. Hynek at the time was an astronomer at Northwestern University. He later became convinced that UFOs are real, and founded his own investigative agency, which took over NICAP's files after that group folded. Thanks to Hynek, a Northwestern University committee and the Air Force's Technical Intelligence Center analyzed one of Simonton's pancakes and found it to be made of flour, sugar and grease; it was rumored, however, that the wheat in the pancakes was of an unknown type.

The official Air Force assessment of it all: This case is unexplained. "The only serious flaw in the story is the disappearance of the craft in 'two seconds.' The rest of the story did not contain any outrages to physical concepts," reads the report. Simonton "answered questions directly, did not contradict himself, insisted on the facts being exactly as he stated and refused to accept embellishments or modifications. He stated he was sure that we wouldn't believe him but that he didn't care whether he was believed. He stated simply that this happened and that was that."

The private Air Force response was unearthed after a little detective work. It comes from a UFO handbook for Air Force personnel, written by Lloyd Mallan and issued in a popular edition by Science and Mechanics Publishing Co. In the book, Mallan refers to "J.S., a highly regarded, much respected citizen of Eagle River, Wis.—a small rural community noted for its attractiveness to tourists."

(Unless there are more space-pancake recipients in Eagle River than otherwise reported, we can safely see through Mallan's clever attempt at disguise and positively identify "J.S." as Joe Simonton.)

One Air Force investigator, according to Mallan, said that Simonton "appeared quite sincere to me, did not appear to be the perpetrator of a hoax." But an Air Force Aeronautical Systems Division psychiatrist believed that Simonton had suffered a hallucination and subsequent delusion. The Air Technical Intelligence Center investigator said, "cases of this type could be injurious to the mental health of the individual if [he] became upset due to the experience. ... It was pointed out that experiences of this type, hallucinations followed by delusion, are not at all uncommon and especially in rural communities."

Additionally, according to Mallan, the Air Force took to heart an unsubstantiated rumor circulated by, among others, Raymond Palmer, a publisher of pulp flying-saucer and science-fiction magazines. Palmer reported to the Air Force his belief that Simonton had been hypnotized by an Eagle River real estate broker and was fed the pancake story so that he would repeat it and appear truthful. The motivation for this was economic, for the purpose of "a miniature Disneyland that is or was being built in the area."

To understand how incredible the rumor was, it is useful to look at the credibility of Palmer himself. One of his favorite theories was that flying saucers came from a secret hollow-Earth civilization ruled by a race called Detrimental Robots, which he abbreviated as "Deros." According to Palmer, the Deros manipulated humanity with their projected thought rays. Palmer's primary source—actually, his only source—was a Pennsylvania welder who drew upon "racial memory" for his accounts. (There apparently is no mention in Air Force files of the possibility that the Deros' thought ray had been turned upon real estate agents, or Palmer, or even the Air Force, though I believe there is as much evidence for that as for an Eagle River Disneyland.)

But based on such sound "evidence," the Air Technical Intelligence Center, which headquartered Air Force UFO investigations, let the matter drop. Publicly, it was a mystery. The classified reason, revealed to Mallan, was that the Air Force would not pursue the matter "due to the possibility of causing [Simonton] embarrassment which might prove injurious to his health." This was an uncharacteristic kindness on the part of the Air Force; they regularly had been dismissing reports from pilots—even their own—as misidentifications or, worse, hallucinations. "There are sufficient psychological explanations for reports not otherwise explainable," concluded the Psychology Branch of the Air Force's Aeromedical Laboratory in 1949. Pilots, police, professors, besides regular folks—all nuts. In the '60s, though, for a brief, shining moment, the Air Force took on a human face and bit its collective tongue, bending over backwards to carry the case of a part-time Santa and full-time chicken farmer as unexplained. Some might smell a conspiracy here.

Conspiracies notwithstanding, it is easy to dismiss Simonton's wrought-iron Italians and their interest in breakfast and farming. But since then a number of arguments have been put forward to explain bizarre alien behavior, especially the alleged alien abductions. The encounters are, perhaps, alien sociology experiments, and we are the subjects. The goal is to elicit an emotional response from the subject, which the aliens study.

"The witness may offer as 'proof' of his experience a couple of pancakes given to him by extraterrestrials, a recitation of meaningless messages, or a story of sexual contact with a girl from outer space," said French UFO researcher Jacques Vallee, a former NASA consultant. "In any case, a pursuit of the rational study of the case is impossible."

Yes, no and maybe. In the early '60s, American farms and farming were of undeniable interest to the alleged aliens. Besides Simonton, for example, there is dairy farmer Gary T. Wilcox, of Tioga City, N.Y. On April 24, 1964, he saw a UFO in his field. Its crew was taking soil samples. He approached the aliens, and they somehow made it known to Wilcox that they would very much like some fertilizer, of all things. They "told" him nonverbally that they were interested in our agricultural practices. The craft departed as Wilcox went to fetch a sack of fertilizer, but he left the fertilizer in the field anyway. The next day it was gone.

Earlier, on June 20, 1953, John Q. Black and John Van Allen observed a UFO crew, dressed similarly to those Simonton saw, scoop a bucket of water and return to their craft, at Brush Creek, Calif. As the UFO left, it made a sound like "steam coming out of a boiler"—not unlike Simonton's description of the sound his UFO made, of "knobby tires on wet pavement."

As for Simonton himself, in the end he was left with a bitter taste in his mouth, and it wasn't from the pancakes. "I haven't been able to work for three weeks," he told United Press International. "I'm going to have to start making some money." He said that the next time he saw a flying saucer he would keep it to himself.

He lied. In 1970 Simonton was visited by Lee Alexander, a UFO enthusiast active in a Detroit-based investigative group. Simonton told Alexander that he had had more visits from the aliens, but he had not told anyone because of the way his first report had been received.

And that is all we know.

BIGFOOT
(AND WEREWOLVES?)
IN OUR BACK YARD

"**J**ust in the outer fringes of the headlights, not quite out of headlight range, I saw this big hairy thing. It scared the devil out of me. It was probably 7- or 8-feet tall. It was running across [the road], from south to north, and it jumped a 4- or 5-foot barbed-wire fence."

The story of what Dennis Fewless saw near Delavan, in Walworth County, late that night in July 1964, is just one of many Wisconsin sightings of a large animal-like creature that walks upright. The creature has dented cars, slashed livestock, hunted hunters and even flown a UFO—if all witnesses are to be believed.

"I'm no nut," Fewless told me. "I'd been making that same drive night after night. It wasn't just a one-night affair. I know what to look for. You know what deer look like or skunk or bear—you know what that looks like. This didn't look anything like that at all. As far as I'm concerned it was real, and no one can tell me it wasn't."

A Delavan native, Fewless was driving home around midnight from his job at the Admiral Television Corp. in Harvard, Ill. After turning onto Highway 89 from Highway 14, his headlights picked up an animal running across the road, from one field to another, on two legs. It was dark colored and weighed between 400 and 500 pounds.

"I was awful scared that night," Fewless told me. "That was no man. It was all hairy from feet to head."

The next day Fewless and his wife returned to look for footprints or other evidence. The sun-baked ground offered no clues, "But we found where the corn had been pushed back aside," he said.

Primarily identified with the Pacific Coast, Wisconsin's Bigfoot would seem far from home. But it's been seen many times in the Great Lakes region; in fact, European immigrants to America first encountered the creature in the Midwest, not the West. In Michigan City, Ind., in the summer of 1839, a "wild child" reportedly haunted that city's Fish Lake, "setting up the most frightful and hideous yells," according to an early press account.

In Wisconsin, it was a "wild man" that in August 1899 was captured in the woods of Chippewa County. The wild man was placed in the county jail. The *Wisconsin State Journal* reported that he "has lost nearly all resemblance to a human being. ... It is impossible to hold a conversation with him as he has lost all knowledge of speech." Residents had reported seeing the wild man for 10 years.

In August 1900, the *State Journal* reported, "A wild man is terrorizing the people north of Grantsburg [in Burnett County]. He appears to be about 35 years of age, has long black whiskers, is barefooted, has scarcely any clothes on him, and he carries a hatchet. He appeared at several farmhouses and asked for something to eat. He secretes himself in the woods all day and has the most blood-curdling yells that have ever been heard in the neighborhood."

While the creature in the latter incident sounds more like a man than a beast, the next sighting includes a more standard Bigfoot description. In 1910, at Mirror Lake in Sauk County, a 10-year-old girl saw a creature in the woods that looked somewhat like a man but was covered with fur. It peacefully trailed her home, leaving tracks twice as large as her father's.

Here are more sightings:

- Nov. 30, 1968, Deltox Marsh near Fremont, Waupaca County: A group of 12 hunters, including Bob Parry, Dick Bleier and Bill Mall or Mallo (accounts differ), had arranged themselves in a line, to drive deer before them. In succession, from left to right, they viewed a powerfully built creature with short, dark brown hair and a hairless face passing before them. It seemed to be watching them, moving forward as they backed off. It finally left. The hunters later said that they would have shot the creature except that it looked too much like a man. It left tracks in the snow, which were photographed. The tracks gave serious researchers pause: They had three toes and appeared to be webbed.

- August 1970, Benton, Lafayette County: About 15 people saw a 7-foot apelike creature with white hair, pink eyes and claws.
- Summer 1992, Jefferson County: Tom Brichta and Chris Maxwell of Hanover Park, Ill., were driving late one foggy night on Highway 106 when they smelled a "skunky" odor. Immediately afterward they spotted a hand sticking into the road. As they passed, they saw the creature it was attached to.

"It was large," said Brichta. "Its lower chest and upper belly was at the top of my car. It was huge, it was hairy, and it was standing over a roadkill."

They slowed and the figure lunged at the vehicle, leaving two scratches. "I've seen plenty of bears, and this wasn't a bear," said Brichta. Two months later, Brichta saw the creature again with Scott Freimund, driving along the same spot. It was 7- to 8-feet tall and was walking on the balls of its feet along the edge of a cornfield, checking between the rows. "It reminded me of a person window-shopping," Brichta said.

The men slowed the car and the creature turned. "It almost seemed to challenge us, like it was saying, 'What are you going to do about it?' " Finally the creature entered the cornfield and disappeared from view. Checking back later, Brichta and his friend found a 5-foot circle of grass—trampled-down grass.

There's a long Native American record of similar encounters. Wisconsin's earliest residents not only believed in this manlike creature, they claimed direct contact with it. It was the Chippewa who named it "Windigo."

"The Windigo are powerful giants," wrote Charles Brown, a historian who collected Windigo stories, in 1927. They were part animal, wild "men" who left footprints twice the normal size. The legends reported that the Windigo killed Indians for food, cut them up and boiled them in their kettles. "The belief in them still persists," Brown wrote.

Who were the Windigo? The Delaware Indians called creatures like them Alligewi, after the Allegheny River. It was the Delaware's belief that the creatures originally had come from the Midwest. The Delaware went to war with the Alligewi as the creatures crossed their territories. The Delaware supposedly fought the Alligewi down the Ohio River, then up the Mississippi and then to Minnesota. The Minnesota Sioux have a legend about a race of giants that appeared there—and were killed.

Nor were the Windigo welcome in Wisconsin. Stories from the state's Chippewa range from fantastic to plausible. While modern sightings usually consist of little more than brief, visual contact, the Chippewa occasionally spoke to the Windigo. In fact, the social structures of the Windigo were known to them. Windigo, for instance, had families, with brothers, sisters and wives. A Windigo and an Indian could even marry, though as a rule the couple would not be welcome in the village.

From Charles Brown's collection of Windigo legends:

"A good many years ago there was a large Indian village. In it were a hundred or more bark-covered wigwams. A Windigo went to this village and killed all the Indians. He left only one woman, whom he wanted for a wife. He didn't eat all the Indians, but cached many of them away for the winter. An Indian who was away from the village hunting rabbits saw the Windigo's tracks. These he followed, and killed the Windigo. He married the woman the Windigo spared."

Other stories are less romantic. A Windigo once stalked an Indian village, catching a man or woman every day or so. The village was soon terrorized. The Windigo then moved near a different village, possibly because residents of the first were staying close to home. At the neighboring village the Indians joined together and hunted the Windigo while he slept. They surprised him and attacked him with axes. After a hard struggle, during which several Indians were killed, the Windigo was destroyed.

Perhaps the most interesting account of the Windigo is the story of a group of castaway Indians who befriend the creatures, later escaping on a passing ship.

Instead of being set in the misty, nonspecific time of legend, this story is fixed firmly as occurring after the arrival of Europeans to

Wisconsin.

"Four Indian families left their camp for the summer," Brown wrote. "They made a big boat with a sail. They sailed for a long time and finally reached an island, where they landed. When they left the boat, a large number of Windigo came and wished to kill them. But the Indians gave them rings and brooches and made friends with them. The Windigo killed a deer and gave it to the Indians. The Indians lived on the island a long time.

"One day they saw a ship. They waved a blanket and it came to the island. The Windigos were sorry to see the Indians leave. They wanted to get into the ship, but the white men on the ship were afraid of them. But for the gifts, the Windigos would have killed and eaten the Indians."

Is the Chippewa Windigo today's Bigfoot? That depends in large part on what we mean by "Bigfoot." It's only been since the 1960s, with the publicity given to Pacific Coast reports, that the creature figuring in regional stories across the United States has been given that general and derisive name.

But the stories, if true, may not all relate to the same creature. Bigfoot, or creatures like Bigfoot, seem to exhibit regionally peculiar behavior. Sometimes physical traits are described that do not fit in well with the standardized portrait. The Pacific Coast Bigfoot is a gentle apelike creature standing around 8 feet tall. It is almost exclusively reported walking upright, leaving large five-toed footprints, averaging 17 inches long.

In Wisconsin, we have reports that fit that. We also have reports of a doglike creature of somewhat smaller stature, who tends to walk upright but who seems to walk on all fours as well. We have other reports of three-toed tracks left by much smaller creatures (these will be dealt with in a separate chapter). It could be, of course, that all of these reports are of the same family of creatures, with differences of size, age and behavior complicating attempts at identification.

Wisconsin's most recent and best-investigated stories of upright monsters are reported by witnesses who describe a living, breathing werewolf. While the creature bears little resemblance to the beast of classic myth, the "werewolf" label has stuck, and what it lacks in tradition it makes up for in terror. It is said to be large. It is fast. And, if it is actually Bigfoot, it is unusually bloodthirsty.

Of course, it could be a real werewolf. That possibility is just the sort of thing that gives researchers fits. While it is slightly feasible that a large primate like Bigfoot could survive, unknown to science, on the densely forested Pacific Coast, it seems a bit far-fetched to believe that such a cliche-ridden bogeyman as a werewolf could be alive in America's Dairyland.

But, it could very well be. First, though, you have to get past the pop culture image of the Hollywood half-man/half-wolf, and explore the early written records. Researcher Daniel Cohen has discovered that in the Middle Ages many supposed werewolves were actually captured and executed. But some met a more fortunate fate. Brought before the courts, magistrates determined that what they were actually dealing with were victims of mental illness. One judge, in fact, sentenced a self-confessed werewolf to confinement in a monastery, because the so-called monster was merely "stupid and idiotic."

Still, there is no rational way to explain the Beast of Le Gevaudan. In mid-July 1764, a young girl was found murdered in the village of St. Etienne de Ludgares, in south-central France. Her heart had been torn out. Several more children died under similar circumstances within the next few days. In late August, shepherds from the village of Langogne reported seeing a creature that walked on two legs. It was entirely covered with short, reddish hair, and its face was "piglike," though they may have made that comparison merely to draw attention to the bluntness of the snout. In a period drawing, the head is distinctly wolfish. The creature was, of course, blamed for the children's deaths.

A man named Jean-Pierre Pourcher, known for his truthfulness, claimed to have shot at the creature. Finally, the king dispatched the militia to track down whatever it was that was terrorizing his countryside. Soldiers arrived in February 1765. They shot at the creature but did not kill it. The murders continued throughout the spring.

A second military expedition in June 1767 killed a large wolf. But it wasn't until June 19 that villagers surrounded what they believed was the true beast, in the woods at Sogne d'Auvert. It was killed with a silver bullet, of course, and the corpse was brought to town. The creature was described as a large and strange-looking wolf, with close-cropped ears and "hooflike" feet. The gun that brought the beast down is still displayed in the church at St. Martin de Bourchaux. The corpse was similarly displayed ... until it spoiled. Then it was buried in an unknown location.

Too hard to believe? Then try this one:

A werewolf seeks out a lonely farmhouse. It attempts entry, terrorizing the woman inside. Later it returns to horribly wound one of the farm animals. Once again the government's leader sends assistance, but it is of little help.

That story comes not from France, but from Wisconsin. David Gjetson officially investigated it as an employee of the Wisconsin Department of Natural Resources in 1972.

"A telephone call was relayed to us from the [Jefferson County] Sheriff's Department," he told me. "They said they had a call from a lady. A large, unknown animal had approached her house and attempted to get in by rattling the door." The house was three or four miles east of Fort Atkinson, in a rural section of Jefferson County.

"It had happened before, but [the creature] had never tried to get in," the DNR investigator said. "Some weeks later, the same beast returned. It had long black hair and was 8 feet tall. It was walking upright, like a man.

"The arms were long, and there was a long claw on each hand. It didn't come to the house, but went to a shed where a horse was. It took a swat at the horse and left a gash across the chest—30 inches from one shoulder to the other." Whatever it was, it left a footprint more than a foot long.

Such aggressive behavior is not typical of Bigfoot, though I am not prepared to start sorting my monsters into different piles: werewolves to the left, Bigfoot (feet?) to the right. For now, for me, it's enough to collect the reports and wonder.

However, violence is common to reports from neighboring Walworth County. Linda Godfrey, a reporter for *The Week*, a county newspaper there, has collected werewolf stories for that region that date back 40 years. Her reports have been featured on the television show, "Inside Edition."

"Some see it on two legs and some see it on four," Godfrey said of the Walworth werewolf. "But the ones who see it on four almost always say it is running differently [from other four-legged animals], covering a great deal more ground than you'd expect."

A typical encounter occurred early in 1992. Two Elkhorn women, Lori Endrizzi and Doris Gipson, were traveling in a car on Bray Road when they saw it. It had large teeth; its eyes reflected the headlights. In the excitement, the women felt the car lurch. They had struck something. Then the animal chased the car. It leapt onto the trunk and left "deep claw marks."

Bigfoot or werewolf? Or something else?

Cherilynn Smage saw something fairly different from Bigfoot in the fall of 1991. She was driving through the tractor lane of a cornfield, taking dinner to her husband. The farm was on Bray Road, in Walworth County. Suddenly she saw a four-legged coyote sort of creature.

"It was staring at me, on all fours," she said, and yet it stood higher than the hood of her Ford Escort. It fled into the woods.

Robert Bushman and his wife saw something similar on Nov. 30, 1991. They were driving on Highway 11 between Elkhorn and Delavan. It was bright and sunny. They saw a deer. They thought it was a deer. Then they thought it was—well, a wolf, but it was too large to be a wolf. It "had a terribly unkempt look to its fur, wild, not normal. It was black, scraggly looking, like no animal." It ran away on all fours.

And as if that were not enough, one night in 1936, just east of Jefferson near Highway 18, Mark Schackelman encountered a talking Windigo/Bigfoot/werewolf.

His son, Joe, editor and publisher of the Kenosha Labor newspaper, recalled, "He came upon the thing digging in an old Indian burial mound."

It was more than 6 feet tall and smelled like decaying meat. Its hair was black, and it had a shriveled thumb and forefinger, giving it a three-fingered appearance. Its ears were pointed and it had a muzzle, "somewhere between a dog and an ape," the younger Schackelman said.

Mark Schackelman saw it again the next night, and this time he heard it speak in a "neo-human" voice.

"My father's first thought was that it must be something satanic, so immediately prayed, and he said it seemed to show some fear at that," Joe Schackelman said. As the creature and Schackelman slowly backed away from each other, the monster "made a three-syllable growling noise that sounded like 'gadara,'* with the emphasis on the second syllable."

This occurred just two miles from Dennis Fewless' 1964 sighting.

Finally, we have the strangest sighting of all. At about 10:30 p.m.

---

* Did Schackelman properly render the muttered speech of the creature? "Gadara" sounds like the name applied to a similar creature found in the northeastern United States. There it is called Garuda, after a flying god in East Indian mythology. To me, the similarity of the words is striking. I don't know if it is significant, but it certainly is curious.

on Dec. 2, 1974, near Frederic in Polk County, William Bosak, a 69-year-old dairy farmer, was driving home when he saw a disc-shaped craft beside the road. "I can remember it just as if it were yesterday," Bosak told me.

The lower half of the craft was shrouded in mist. It had a curved glass window, and inside the brightly lit compartment Bosak saw a creature covered with dark tan fur, except for its face and chin.

"He was looking out the window, and it was a different kind of character than you'd see on this earth," he said. "It looked a good deal like a man, but it had a different-looking face than you'd see. It had a kind of a cow-looking face."

Asked to elaborate, Bosak explained that the face

This talking creature was encountered twice near Jefferson in 1936 by Mark Schackelman. At his direction, his son, Joe, sketched this likeness. (Courtesy Joe Schackelman)

had hair on its sides. The ears stuck out from the head about three inches, and the eyes were large and protruding.

The creature held its arms above its head, and its expression led Bosak to believe that it was "just as scared as I was." After about 10 seconds Bosak quickly drove away, and as he did so his car lights dimmed, the engine sounded as if it were missing, and he heard a soft "whooshing" noise.

The next day Bosak returned to the area and found a round spot, 6 feet in diameter, pressed down into the hayfield.

"There are other people that had seen something like that," said

Bosak, "right in this area."

This is the best, and one of the least sensational, of the very rare sightings linking Bigfoot-like creatures with UFOs. It is also the least publicized.

"You know how the neighbors are," Bosak said. "They questioned it. The editor in town didn't believe it. You know, though, something? If you've ever thought of outer space—it's just fantastic, isn't it? A lot of people can imagine such things.

"But this is a fact."

Well!

What is it? And what does this thing have against cars?

Scratches are nice but hardly conclusive, as far as proof is concerned. As for other proof, Linda Godfrey has noted that the reports we have collected between us almost all take place near the western and southern edges of the Kettle Moraine State Forest. And, as you'll find later, this is a small hotspot of UFO activity. But I have no explanation for this, and I tend not to like explaining one unexplained phenomenon in terms of another.

Ignoring for the moment that what we have here may be an alien or some sort of organic robot doing the aliens' bidding (a theory sometimes proposed in joint UFO-Bigfoot sightings), the skeptic's response often is this: If these things are real, why haven't we ever found their remains?

The answer is that we might have.

Aborigines of Minnesota, a report of the Minnesota Geological Survey, brought news in 1888 of an excavation of Indian mounds near La Crescent, across the Mississippi from La Crosse. A large copper skillet was found, and "bones of men of huge stature."

Other Minnesota Indian mound excavations revealed additional evidence: On Aug. 12, 1896, the *St. Paul Globe* reported that "a huge man" was dug up on the Beckley farm on Lake Koronis. At Moose Island Lake, remains of 7-foot men were found; near Pine City, "outlandish skeletons"; in Warren, in 1882, 10 "gigantic bodies"; at Chatfield, seven 8-foot skeletons, with skulls showing receding foreheads, the mouths full of double rows of teeth.

As impossible as it may seem, could it be that the Chippewa Windigo stories are true? Did Indian and monster coexist in prehistory? And if we grant that the physical evidence is suggestive, dare we link these monsters to similar creatures seen on the West Coast today?

Consider this: Another Indian mound—the Grand Mound, in Itasca, Minn.—yielded 100 skeletons, some more than 10 feet tall. And they were found with sea shells native to the Pacific Ocean.

OF KANGAROOS AND CHUPACABRAS

Quick: Which is easier for you to believe has been seen in Wisconsin—Bigfoot or kangaroos? And what if those kangaroos were responsible for some of Wisconsin's mysterious animal deaths?

"Well ...," you are probably thinking, "there just might be something to this Bigfoot thing."

Actually, both these creatures have been spotted here, though kangaroos may have been mistaken for Bigfoot. Or both may be something else—something that would explain some of the livestock mutilations.

Wisconsin kangaroo reports date back to 1899, and they rival Bigfoot reports in number. The more recent sightings:

On April 5, 1978, two people spotted a kangaroo in Waukesha at 6:45 a.m., on East Moreland Boulevard.

Was it an optical illusion?

At 6:15 p.m. April 12, Jill and Peter Haeselich spotted one from their Pewaukee dining room. Peter even chased it. "It was going pretty quick," Jill told a reporter. "It was hopping. We knew it had to be a kangaroo."

A hoax?

At 4:45 p.m. April 13, Waukesha County social worker William J. Busch was driving home on Highway 83 when he saw a 3-foot creature with an "odd-shaped" head, small front legs and long back feet, scampering across the road, 15 feet away.

At 3 a.m. April 16, Greg and Janet Napientek saw a kangaroo as they were driving on County A, east of Waukesha.

Beginning to think something might be out there? All right, there could possibly be a single, escaped kangaroo in Wisconsin. Just one. A fluke.

At about 10:45 a.m. April 23, Lance and Loretta Nero saw two kangaroos from their hilltop home on Sierra Drive in Brookfield. The Waukesha County Sheriff's Department found tracks, which they said had possibly been made by deer or cows.

Mark Hall, who investigates sightings of strange and apparently misplaced animals, checked into the report. He told his fellow "crypto-zoologist," Loren Coleman, that the Neros were bright and sincere. Hall saw the casts that the Neros had made of the tracks. They were around 6 inches long and 3 inches wide. "Generally the tracks have a two-pronged-fork appearance with two knobs at the rear of the 'fork handle,' " Hall said. "The tracks were impressed into mud at a new housing development, which accounts for the depth of them."

I have seen photos of the casts, and I believe they could possibly account for the bizarre "three-toed" webbed tracks left by some of the creatures reported as Bigfoot in Wisconsin. In this case, the depth of the tracks may also be due to the creature's great weight.

At 2:30 a.m. April 24, Tom Frank saw a kangaroo near County C in Merton. On May 9 one was sighted at Camelot Forest, a Waukesha housing development. On May 21, in Eau Claire County, a woman saw one on Highway 12 between Augusta and Fall Creek. Finally, in case there are still any doubters out there, at 5:20 p.m. April 24, something like a kangaroo was photographed near Waukesha, near county highways SS and M.

Two 23-year-old Menomonee Falls men saw the creature and took two SX-70 Polaroid color photos. They have refused to give reporters permission to print their names, but the clearer of their photos has been reprinted as far away as England's *Fortean Times*, a journal of unexplained phenomena. And it is reprinted here.

Loren Coleman, who collated these Wisconsin kangaroo reports, says the photo shows "a tan animal with lighter-brown front limbs, hints of a lighter-brown hind limb, dark-brown or black patches around the eyes, inside the two upright ears and possibly surrounding the nose and upper-mouth area." He compares it favorably to the wallaby, or brush kangaroo, native to Tasmania where it ranges from lower valleys to snowy summits—ahem—such as might be found in Wisconsin.

Kangaroos, or something like them, have appeared in other parts of the central United States. Two kangaroos were sighted near the Anoka County Fairgrounds near Coon Rapids, Minn., from 1957 to 1967. In January 1934, an incredibly fast kangaroo attacked dogs, geese and ducks in rural Tennessee. The *Chattanooga Daily Times* concluded, "There is absolutely no doubt about these facts. A kangaroo-like beast visited the community and killed dogs ... and that's all there is to it."

Impossible?

Perhaps. And it would be nice to leave the matter there, nice to think that, along with Wisconsin's alleged sightings of lake monsters, ghosts and Bigfoot, there also come sightings of friendly, but no less mysterious, creatures as well.

But along came the Chupacabras.

The Chupacabras, or "goat-sucker," made its mysterious debut in Puerto Rico in 1995. Since then it has been reported in Florida, Massachussetts, New York, New Jersey, Texas and California. Whatever the truth of the matter is, it is blamed for leaving a trail littered with dead livestock. That much is established fact. Part of the puzzle is that there is no established tradition of the Chupacabras. Things like lake monsters, Bigfoot, vampires and so on have a long history. If we didn't call them by the names we have today, at least there is a suggested counterpart in folklore. Not so with the Chupacabras. It seems to have come out of nowhere, leading some to theorize that it is an escaped genetic experiment, or an alien creature sent to demonize us, or both.

The Chupacabras has been seen by various people, including Puerto Rican officials. It attacks livestock, puncturing the necks, suggesting that it may feed on its victim's blood. The marks are made by the upper teeth. There are no corresponding marks showing similar teeth on the lower jaw. The description of the creature varies. It is a child's sort of animal, made up of dissimilar animal parts; it has feathers, like a bird; or it has fur, like a mammal; or it has scales, like a lizard; or bumps, like a frog. It is upright. It has small arms and hands. It has a muzzle. It is gray. And/or it has red feathers, from the neck down. It has tiny, pointed ears and large, wrap-around eyes. It has claws, like the creature that swatted the horse in Fort Atkinson. Some "Chupas" reports make it out to be a 7- or 8-foot Bigfoot, but most often it sounds a lot like a kangaroo—a mean kangaroo.

In Sweetwater, Fla., where it was seen in March 1996, it was described as "a doglike figure standing up, with two short hands in the air." In May 1996, it was seen in Arizona, where it apparently "mumbled and gestured." In June 1996, it was spotted in the Sonora Desert of Mexico, where witnesses described it as "like a turkey or kangaroo." In fact, in the Campo Rico district of Puerto Rico, it is not called Chupacabras at all, but is referred to as "el canguro." Guess what that translates as?

Bigfoot, kangaroo, werewolf or "Chupacabras"? Whatever it is, this upright creature was observed by many in Waukesha County in 1978 and was captured on two Polaroid color photos. (Courtesy Loren Coleman)

In all, whatever its skin is like, it is shaped like a kangaroo. Its tracks show three toes, with webbed feet. One report has it able to jump a 6-foot fence.

And it does not walk or run.

It hops.

I am not so sure that what I have is a photo of a Wisconsin kangaroo, and it may be that the Chupas did not come out of nowhere after all.

CATTLE
MUTILATIONS

Cattle mutilations are perhaps the oddest of unexplained phenomena. While other events—sightings of UFOs, ghosts and so on—typically are stories with no physical evidence, the mutilation of livestock provides grisly physical evidence in abundance but no accompanying narrative.

In the most classic examples, one or more beef carcasses are found with organs removed with surgical precision. There are no signs of a death struggle, nor are there footprints or tire tracks nearby. Despite the profound mystery and lack of real clues in classic cattle mutilations, some observers have blamed UFOs, blood cults and even military intelligence agencies with black, unmarked helicopters.

There have been a number of reported cattle mutilations in Wisconsin: in Lincoln County in August 1978; near Patch Grove, in Grant County, in November 1976; and near Eastman, in Crawford County, in October 1975. In the Patch Grove incident, a Holstein cow was mutilated on the farm of Jerry and Ivan Schmidt. In Eastman, six Hereford cattle were mutilated. In Lincoln County, an ear and lip were taken from a cow.

For current information and an overall perspective on this international phenomena, we must momentarily leave the Midwest and travel to Fyffe, Ala., where one of the best and most recent official investigations occurred. In 1993, the local police department released its report. It serves as an accurate portrait of cattle mutilations in general: "To date, over 30 animals have been discovered dead in pastures with various internal and external organs missing. The incisions examined on these animals exhibit a precise surgical cutting. In many of the cases, there has been evidence of extremely high heat at the tissue excisions. The absence of physical evidence adds to the mystery at the majority of mutilation sites. Though many animals have been found in soft pasture land, and in many cases mud, there have been no footprints, tracks, or marks found anywhere near the mutilated animals.

"To date, no police agency has established a suspect or motive for these incidents of phantom surgery perpetrated on area livestock. ... Comparison to other cattle mutilations documented by law enforcement in 48 other states since 1963 shows that the cases recently documented here in northeast Alabama are part of a national problem. In over 10,000 reported cases of livestock mutilations reported since 1967, the organs and tissue taken are always the same: sex organs removed, tongue cut deep into the throat and removed; individual eyes and ears or sometimes both have been excised; the jaw stripped to the bone in a large oval cut and all tissue cut clean; rectums are cored out, almost like a stovepipe had been inserted and all the tissue and muscle has been pulled out.

"All of this has been accomplished on these thousands of animals with no evidence of blood present at the incision. In some cases, the entire blood supply of the animal had been drained, yet without cardiovascular collapse.

"Throughout the documented history of these cattle mutilations, no one has ever been charged or prosecuted with the crime. No one has ever been caught."

Records at the Wisconsin Animal Health Laboratories, a cooperative program of the Wisconsin and U.S. Departments of Agriculture, are sadly incomplete. The Animal Health Laboratories responded to only one mutilation report I know of, that from the sheriff of Crawford County, which I believe related to the 1975 Eastman incident. The autopsy report survives. The primary diagnostician was Dr. Armin

Krohn, who personally viewed the wooded, hilly pasture where four Hereford beef cows were found. All the cows were mutilated, and the bodies had suffered from decomposition.

From Krohn's report: "At least one cow showed evidence of knife work, which I readily duplicated with my necropsy knife." Additionally, "All cows showed evidence of scavenger feeding (crows, coyotes, dogs, etc.)." Krohn was unable to determine the cause of death. The location, positioning of the bodies and lack of ground markings showed that the deaths had occurred quickly. Krohn found no evidence that the deaths were caused by a cult, UFO or anything else "abnormal," though some might find his own theory just as unusual: "One would have no difficulty producing these particular death losses—which occurred within a 24-hour period—with the use of a dart gun," he wrote. Krohn reported that there had been other "mysterious" cattle deaths in the area but they later had been found to have been caused by infectious disease or metabolic problems.

In December 1992, a series of livestock deaths vaguely similar to cattle mutilations was reported near Cottage Grove, in Dane County. Wild dogs, coyotes and even cougars were suspected—all with no real evidence. At the farm of Roger and Ann Gausmann, 14 goats were killed or missing. The Dane County Sheriff's Department believed that a pack of feral dogs was responsible. "They become instant predators as soon as they get in a pack," said a spokesman. "They don't kill for food, but for excitement, and then they go home." The sheriff's department did not explain why dogs killing for excitement would remove carcasses, or what they would do with them. "I have no idea why [the mutilators] came or what they were," said Ann Gausmann, but she was relieved when the attacks stopped.

Wild dogs and coyotes were also blamed for unusual livestock deaths in Grant County in November 1981. Packs of feral dogs were actually observed chasing livestock. Liberty Township Constable Jane Weber said that the dogs also had been eating animals caught in hunters' traps. In Stitzer, farmer Willi Maier blamed coyotes for the death of one of his registered Suffolk ewes. He'd already lost nine lambs in June. In Hazel Green, Pat Birkett said he was raccoon hunting when he encountered a pack of 15 wild dogs. His own hunting dogs fought them off while Birkett ran for his car. The tame dogs, he said, came out of it "pretty chewed up."

Other tame dogs at the time seemed to catch the same feral excitement. Coreen Kitto of rural Lancaster was bringing her husband, John, home from the hospital. As the Kittos left their car for the house, their neighbor's two Great Danes ran across the field toward them. "One of them came right at John," Coreen Kitto recalled. "I got my husband's crutches and beat the dogs off."

The existence of packs of wild dogs is feasible, according to the state Department of Natural Resources. DNR specialist Chuck Pills notes that coyotes do breed with dogs, and that their offspring can be quite large. He cites the example of what seemed to be the body of a large German shepherd, recovered in Green County in the mid-1970s. "Tests showed that the animal was a coyote," Pills says.

Other government agencies are not as ready to accept such prosaic answers. Back in Fyffe, Ala., an investigation of a mutilated black Angus cow in January 1993 "revealed a flaky white material on the animal's right rib cage and on the ground 5 feet from the carcass," states the police report. The material was placed in the empty wrapper of a cigarette pack and transported to the department. While removing the flaky particles from the cigarette wrapper, the material came in contact with the brass tip of a ball-point pen.

"Within one second of contact with the brass, the material melted into an almost clear liquid," the report goes on to say. "To reduce the risk of this happening to the remaining material, the rest was shaken out into a jar where it remained unaffected. This white, flaky material was then Air Expressed to a molecular biologist at a leading Eastern university for analysis. After two tests, the scientist determined that the substance was composed of aluminum, titanium, oxygen and silicon in significant amounts. He stated that the amount of titanium was larger than he would ever expect to see in any substance and that there was no way this combination of elements could ever occur in nature."

LAKE MONSTERS: THE ONES THAT GOT AWAY

I have discovered that people pretty much take anything in stride.

You might assume that if a town had a monster, it would be a well-known monster, a marvelous thing. Locals would click their tongues and point to the place where the monster was sighted and say, "Yeah, that's right there where it happened." People would remember for generations.

But people do not. There is minor awareness for a few years, then everyone gets back to business.

The best example of this blase attitude concerns Wisconsin's lakes. At one time or another, many Wisconsin lakes have boasted their very own saurian monster. In 1867, for example, Lake Michigan's sightings were so convincing that the *Chicago Tribune* announced, "that Lake Michigan is inhabited by a vast monster, part fish and part serpent, no longer admits of doubt." But despite the publicity lake monster stories once received, today they are largely forgotten.

Wisconsin's water creatures were known to the Indians long before white settlers came into the area. While we may not have proof of the serpents themselves, we have proof of earlier residents' belief in

27

them. The prehistoric mound-builders—whoever they were—built earthen effigies in the monsters' honor. The later Woodland Indians made offerings to the beasts, sprinkling tobacco on the waters. The Winnebago Indians believed in two kinds of lake creatures: "Wak Tcexi" and "Winnebozho." Wak Tcexi was a spirit, a bad one. Winnebozho was a real animal, the Winnebago thought, physically similar to Wak Tcexi but harmless.

Though they were spirits, the Wak Tcexi had real actions; they were said to have long tails and evil moods, sometimes overturning Indian canoes and drowning the natives. At night, so went the legends, the creatures would climb the banks and come ashore. In the Indian pantheon, these evil spirits frequently battled with the benign Thunderbirds.

The most recent reported sighting of a Wisconsin lake monster was in July 1943. Joseph Davis, today a resident of Galveston Bay, Texas, was 15 years old when he went out to fish on Rock Lake, in his native town of Lake Mills in Jefferson County. He saw a patch of water roiling—the wind, no doubt; but then from out of the water rose the torso of a brownish-black creature. It was 6 or 7 feet long at the surface and who knows how much longer beneath the waves.

For a minute Davis sat in his boat, spellbound, waiting for the head to rise up. But the creature dove down instead, and Davis fled to shore.

As we shall later see, this south-central lake is home to a number of oddities associated with a nearby prehistoric Indian settlement called Aztalan. The origin of the secretive Aztalaners, and their disappearance, was as much a puzzle to the neighboring Woodland Indians as it is to today's archeologists. We do know that the Aztalaners were part of a far-flung trading empire; shells from both the Atlantic and Pacific oceans are among the artifacts that have been recovered from Aztalan. The monster in Rock Lake was supposedly left by the Aztalaners to protect their legacy.

As early as 1867, white settlers believed that there was indeed something unusual in the lake. That year there were a number of sightings. A man named Harbeck saw a "saurian" in the water several times and claimed to have once encountered it on shore, where the creature "hissed at him." Another time it grabbed his trolling hook and pulled his boat along; he believed his escape was miraculous. A Mr. R. Hassam saw the creature in the rushes at lake's edge. At first he thought it was a tree limb. "On closer examination he saw it was a thing of life and stuck it with a spear, but could no more hold it than an ox," reported the local paper. Fred Seaver saw it twice, once after the creature seized his trolling hook and pulled his boat "at a rushing speed" more than half a mile, until Seaver cut the line. Swimmers avoided the lake that year.

The best sighting occurred in 1882. Ed McKenzie and D.W. Seybert were rowing boats on the lake, racing each other to a sandbar. A little ahead they saw what appeared to be a floating log. It proved to be some sort of animal, 3 feet of it above the surface. It opened its mouth about a foot and dove out of sight, only to reappear almost immediately next to McKenzie's craft. McKenzie later stated that it was as long as his boat and that it was the color of a pickerel.

"Strike him with the oar," Seybert yelled, according to the Aug. 31, 1882, issue of the *Lake Mills Spike* newspaper. McKenzie screamed, stood up in his boat and called to shore for help.

"Bring a gun! Bring a gun! There's a big thing out here. Come quick!" he shouted to witnesses on a nearby boat landing. One of them, John Lund, said he clearly saw the creature, though at first he took it to be a man struggling in the water. Lund soon recognized the creature, however, as the one he had encountered while fishing just the week before. It had snapped his trolling line, but not before pulling on it so hard that it cut Lund's hand.

Not all the witnesses agreed that the creature was threatening. Ol Hurd, on the boat landing with Lund, thought it resembled a huge dog. Whatever it was, it looked dangerous to another witness named Wilson. He grabbed a shotgun and took a swift boat to McKenzie and Seybert. But when he arrived the creature had fled.

"The air all around was heavy with a most sickening odor," reported the *Lake Mills Spike*. McKenzie was pale. His teeth were chattering.

Then, as today, witnesses to the incredible sight were taunted; in McKenzie's case, however, it was not the story that was doubted so much as his courage. He hotly replied, "Let them talk about striking it with an oar, or anything. There isn't one of 'em would do it if they'd see it come up sudden like, with its mouth wide open!"

The creature, or family of creatures, was not confined to Rock Lake. Archives at the Historical Society provide clues to monster hot spots.

- Elkhart Lake, Sheboygan County: In the mid-1890s a fisherman went out on a pier to pull up his set line and discovered he had caught something awfully large. He hauled the line back with great effort, finally pulling up something with a large head. It had wide-open eyes and huge jaws. More than that he didn't wait to see. He believed that his escape had been narrow, given the creature's mood. Swimmers avoided that part of the lake for the rest of the season.

- Lake Geneva, Walworth County: In the 1890s, boaters on Geneva Lake, a southeastern resort lake, as well as on nearby Delavan Lake, reported that the water would mysteriously boil up around them, right before they were capsized. The wet vacationers attributed their mishaps to a serpent who could sometimes be seen following in the wake of lake steamboats. It seemed to lurk near an area known as the Narrows and at the Fontana end of the lake.

- Lake Kegonsa, near Stoughton, Dane County: Here the creature was called a dragon. It was seen around Colladay and Williamson Points more than once, and was reported to be quite a bit more mean-spirited than its peers in other lakes.

- Lake Michigan: The earliest sightings by white settlers were made in August 1867. The crews of two boats, the George W. Wood and the Sky Lark, said that they saw a serpentine creature off Evanston, Ill. A fisherman named Joseph Muhike later saw it a mile and a half off Chicago's Hyde Park.

  By the turn of the century, the creature seemed to have moved north, to Milwaukee, where "a ferocious looking beast" was sighted by commercial fishermen. When the men came to shore and reported what they'd seen, they were made fun of, but boaters in the city's bay soon saw it themselves.

  The creature first appeared to be "a large cask." "When they passed near it they saw that it was the head of a large serpentine animal which was floating at rest," wrote Charles Brown, who collected the stories for the State Historical Society of Wisconsin in the 1930s. Whatever the creature was, it was next spotted from Milwaukee's Michigan Street bridge, easing down the Milwaukee River. The man who saw it described a grayish-green serpent, moving downstream. Later the same day it was reported near the river's mouth.

- Oconomowoc Lake, Waukesha County: Here the creature was a

"demon," and sighting reports were collected by Judge Anthony Derse.

- Pewaukee Lake, Waukesha County: In the 1890s, reports were made of "a huge green thing traveling like a gray streak." This particular beast spouted water from its head. A reward was offered for its capture, but fear was so high that no one even tried to collect it. One witness claimed to have thrown a spear at the creature, only to see the weapon rebound from its hide as if it were made of rock or iron.
- Red Cedar Lake, Jefferson County: In 1890, a farmer claimed to have seen a serpent 40 feet long carrying off one of his hogs. In 1891, a serpent was seen by a fisherman tying up his boat. He looked up and saw an undulating body, something like that of a snake. The head he could not see. Farmers and other fishermen claimed to have also observed the serpent; one stated that the creature had a very large head with "protuberances like saw teeth" on its 50-foot back. In 1892, the serpent was blamed for partially devouring five sheep belonging to William Ward. If the reports had been invented to attract tourists, the effort back-fired. Fears were so severe that residents of nearby Lake Ripley, joined to Red Cedar Lake by an underground stream, closed their summer cottages and returned to their homes in the cities.

If you've tried everywhere else, come to the capital city for a monster; 22 witnesses have reported seeing a strange, serpentine monster on Madison's lakes on at least nine separate occasions. Early Madisonians dubbed the monster "Billy Dunn's Sea Serpent," after a letter carrier who claimed to have seen it.

Sightings began in the 1860s, when W.J. Park and his wife were boating near Governor's Island on Lake Mendota. Park was a printer who wrote an early history of Madison. The couple were rowing in a small boat when, as was so often the case, they came alongside what appeared to be a log or piece of driftwood. When Park raised his oar to tap the log, the water suddenly boiled up. The "log" was diving.

"That this was a monster of some sort, we have no doubt," wrote Park. "And we were not too long in deciding that retreat was the better part of valor and we resolved to say nothing about the matter." He and his wife came forward only after others made their own reports.

On July 21, 1892, Darwin Boehmer and a friend saw the creature while they were boating on Lake Monona. Boehmer was the son of a local harness maker. He said that when he and his friend saw the creature it was moving quickly toward Ott's Springs, near Esther Beach on the south shore. The creature passed within 75 feet of them, undulating in an up-and-down motion. Its head, they said, resembled that of a dogfish. Several people on shore at the time also reported seeing the creature, and described its body as 10 to 15 feet long and a foot in circumference.

On Sept. 26, 1892, Joe Daubner, a laundry operator, reported seeing the creature on Lake Monona. On Oct. 7, 1892, an anonymous Oregon resident said he too saw it on Lake Monona, and that he would not go out on the lake again "for all the money in the capital city." He had wanted to go fishing and had hired a boat from John Schott's boat livery. According to the man's story, he rowed out into the lake and the creature passed underneath, apparently trying to turn the boat over. It appeared to be 20 feet long, with a large head that was flat on top. The man dropped his fishing pole and quickly rowed to shore. Once safe, he vowed never to return to the city without a Winchester rifle and two revolvers.

On Oct. 17, 1892, a group of 12 young men saw a 35-foot-long creature once again in Lake Mendota. Around that time, a young man reported encountering the creature in the Yahara River, which links Mendota and Monona. It looked like a log, except that it swam and dove—and tried to overturn his boat.

Five years later, on June 11, 1897, the creature was reported near the eastern shore of Lake Monona. Eugene Heath, a Madison farm machinery salesman, shot at it twice. It turned and came for him. He fled. According to a newspaper headline: "Bullets Had No Effect on Its Hide. Looked Like Bottom of a Boat, But Twice as Long." The paper also reported that "it is probably the same animal which is credited with having devoured a dog which was swimming in the lake a few days ago."

John Schott, owner of the boat livery mentioned above, saw the creature for himself at this time. "He saw it plainly in the bright moonlight, and its shape was like the bottom of a boat, but it was about twice as long. Mr. Schott's two sons saw it, and were so firmly convinced that it was a dangerous animal that when soon after two ladies desired to be rowed over to Lakeside [a resort across the lake], neither of the Schotts, who had spent a large portion of their lives on the lake, would venture out."

If you are in the business of renting pleasure boats, this would seem to be an odd sort of publicity campaign. The Schotts would have done better to keep the sightings to themselves. Yet, all involved told the paper, "Mr. Schott and others who saw the 'thing,' whatever it may be, insist that it is a reality and not a joke or a creature of their combined imaginations."

Two years later, on Aug. 22, 1899, Barney Reynolds reported seeing the creature in Lake Mendota, near the landing for the Bernard Boat Yard. It was also seen in Lake Waubesa, a few miles to the south. An Illinois tourist was anchored in the lake when he saw the water a few hundred feet away begin to heave and swell. A body, then a head, came up—and paused. The creature appeared to be basking in the summer sun; it was 60 to 70 feet long, dark green, with a "serpent head." The tourist tried to decide if it was a fish or an eel or what—and then carefully, gently rowed to shore. There he was called a liar and an alcoholic.

That same summer a man and wife swimming on Waubesa Beach saw the head of an odd creature surface and swim toward them, its eyes glittering. "The couple were good swimmers and did not linger," writes historian Charles Brown.

For these reports I have depended largely on newspaper accounts of the day. There's little doubt that newspaper hoaxes were a well-established tradition in 19th-century journalism. In an age before television and radio, the public enjoyed newspaper hoaxes as recreation. However, the last Madison sightings occurred too late to be explained away as reporters' tall tales.

In the summer of 1917, a fisherman at Picnic Point on Madison's Lake Mendota was the first to see something with "a large snake-like head, with large jaws and blazing eyes." It was less than a hundred feet away. The man was paralyzed at first but then ran away, leaving his pole and catch basket behind. He and his story were ridiculed.

Around the same time, a male and female university student were lying on their backs on a Lake Mendota pier getting a suntan, with their feet hanging over the edge, when the woman felt a sort of tickle on the sole of one foot. It happened a few more times, and she looked at her friend, who she thought was flirting. He was sleeping. She relaxed and closed her eyes. After a time, the tickling began again. Annoyed, she turned over—and saw "a huge snake or dragon" bobbing nearby. The students said "it had a friendly, humorous look in its big eyes," but the two still fled to a nearby fraternity house.

Additional reports were made that summer by bathers and sailors. Overturned canoes and uprooted piers were blamed on the serpent all season. In all, however, the monster was "a rather good-natured animal, playing pranks," in the eyes of Brown, writing little more than a decade after the fact. But, he also noted, "People made more use of the lake after he disappeared."

Were these sightings all hoaxes or misidentifications of more common creatures? I would argue against the possibility of all the reports being hoaxes simply because they are so, well, boring. A made-up story could have provided a lot more description, better action and greater drama. True newspaper hoaxes of the 19th century were carried on for weeks, growing in fantastic detail; after all, the point of the hoax was to build circulation. The longer and better the hoax, the more papers were sold.

As for misidentifications, it's entirely possible that exceptionally large fish survived in Wisconsin's lakes well into the first decades of commercial fishing. A 5-foot muskie actually was caught in Lake Mills in this century—certainly a monster by anyone's definition.

I myself have seen things I cannot immediately explain. But let me stress the word "immediately." Walking along the lakeshore path, on Mendota's southern edge, I have seen blots of dark flesh roiling the water, all in a row, one-two-three. The humps of an undulating serpent? As I watched, and the action repeated, I saw that the humps were fish spawning in the warm shallows.

But compared to the state's early residents, I know nothing of the lakes. They lived on them, measured their days by them, and in many cases made their livings off them. It was a time of ferries and excursion steamers. Appreciation of the landscape was one of the few recreational pastimes available. I think that if they believed they saw something unusual, they saw something unusual.

Skeptics, of course, will set the entire matter aside for a lack of physical evidence.

Well ...

An unusual scale, "of large size, thick and very tough," washed up on the shore of Picnic Point on Madison's Lake Mendota, before the 1917 wave of sightings. Its nature stumped experts at the University of Wisconsin. The State Historical Society records that one anonymous professor, originally from New England, believed the scale belonged to a "sea serpent." And, according to the society, dredging on the same lake, near Madison's Olbrich Park, in the 1890s revealed some "huge vertebrae" belonging to a long-dead, unknown creature.

Theories about similar lake monsters around the world suggest eels, unusually large but otherwise pedestrian fish, and prehistoric creatures ranging from dinosaurs to mammoth invertebrates. In Wisconsin, however, it seems entirely possible to explain the reports in terms of incredibly unlikely yet more reasonable prehistoric survivors: the crocodile and alligator.

Crocodiles or alligators (I prefer not to differentiate based upon the sketchy descriptions) were sighted, and in some cases recovered, on Rock River (which feeds Rock Lake) in 1892, on Manitowoc River in 1978, at a farm pond near Monroe in 1977 and on Pewaukee Lake in 1971.

On Sept. 7, 1996, Madisonian Dan Johnson was fishing on the Wisconsin River, near Ferry Bluff Road in Sauk County, when he actually caught one. Johnson managed to beach the alligator/ crocodile while bystander Kim Cates of Spring Green snapped some pictures of the 3-foot reptile. The creature escaped before Johnson was able to secure it.

If Wisconsin's lake monsters actually are a family of alligators or crocodiles, we might look again at the Indian legend that claims that they were introduced to Rock Lake by that tribe of traders, the Aztalaners. Could those early Wisconsin residents have brought a family of crocodiles here to protect their legacy? And if so, how could the reptiles survive here? While that seems impossible, it's only one of many "impossibilities" centered around Aztalan, as we'll see next.

ATLANTIS IN WISCONSIN

Atlantis, Aztalan, Aztec.

Scuba diver and Atlantis buff Frank Joseph has made an exceptionally strong case for linking these three things using the folklore of three continents. His books, *The Lost Pyramids of Rock Lake* and *Atlantis in Wisconsin*, present a lot of evidence that is circumstantial, and a lot of it that is not.

Atlantis is the legendary utopia that was consumed by the sea prior to Greece's classical era. The Aztecs were the very real race of Indians encountered—and slaughtered—by Cortez in his plunder of the New World. And Aztalan is a prehistoric settlement in Wisconsin, in Jefferson County near Lake Mills. Today it is a state park.

Joseph's theory is that the citizens of Atlantis—located somewhere to the west of the Mediterannean—founded an outpost in Wisconsin, mined copper, cast it into ingots and shipped it to Europe, fueling that continent's Bronze Age. A cataclysm destroyed Atlantis, and survivors in the Wisconsin settlement closed shop and migrated south. After a while they came back to Wisconsin, founded Aztalan and reopened the mines. Then they left once more, created a new

Aztalan in Mexico, and became the Aztecs. (The Aztecs themselves referred to their far-away, long-ago homeland—wherever it was—as "Aztlan.") The first part of this saga, of course, happened centuries before Columbus was alive, or Christ, for that matter.

Wisconsin's Aztalan is a truly bizarre place even if it's not linked to sunken fairytale islands or vanished Mexican Indians. Still, the following are the facts.

Around 3000 B.C., the area that today is Lake Mills was settled by a large number of outsiders. They mined copper in Michigan's Upper Peninsula in the summertime and retired during the winter months to Lake Mills. They buried their dead at Lake Mills, in mounds, and created earthworks aligned for celestial significance.*

Then, in 1198 B.C., they left. A canal dug from the Rock River flooded their sacred necropolis, or "city of the dead," that had been built on the shores of Rock Lake. The water level was raised 60 feet, engulfing all but the tops of the tallest ceremonial structures. (When European settlers came into the area, they observed the stones poking above the water and named it Rock Lake. The Rock River and Rock County were also named for these rocks. Subsequent development raised the water even more, relegating the old settlers' stories to the category of myth. Thanks to Joseph and others, the structures have been rediscovered and firmly established as real.) The visitors moved south. Their journey is recalled by the Attiwandeton and Chippewa, who fought them along the way.

Frank Joseph believes that when the visitors left Wisconsin they traveled to Ecuador. It's not unreasonable to assume that they already had settlements there—they were a far-flung tribe and while in Wisconsin imported seashells from both the Atlantic and Pacific coasts. Around 900 A.D. they returned to the Midwest, creating a huge and complex city at Cahokia in southwest Illinois. Cahokia was abandoned in 1100 A.D., and at least some of the visitors returned to Lake Mills. There they built a miniature Cahokia, a stockaded village where they practiced rites, including cannibalism, that terrified the native Indians. The visitors called their settlement "Aztalan," a name that is gibberish in any Native American tongue but which, they told the

---

* The visitors were not alone in their knowledge of astronomy. Wisconsin's Winnebago Indians possessed a 4½-foot staff, called the *Tshi-zun-hau* stick. Its markings accurately recorded lunar cycles over a two-year period. An example of such a staff is in the collection of Michigan's Cranbrook Institute of Science. In 1985, Alexander Marshack, an archeologist at Harvard University's Peabody Museum, called the staff the "most complex astronomical and problem-solving" device yet found among North American Indians.

Woodland Indians, meant "place by the water." It was a 21-acre sacred center, with housing for the noble class. The bulk of the population lived outside the sacred center. Again these people created huge earthworks, some of them pyramidal, strongly suggestive of the later Aztec pyramids. They also resumed their mining in the Upper Peninsula.

Sometime between 1320 and 1325 A.D., the visitors once again left Wisconsin, once again destroying their settlement before departing. This time instead of water, they used fire. They did not return.

To the native Woodland Indians, the visitors appeared strange. One surviving female skeleton is 5 feet 7 inches tall, which was tall for the time, especially for an Indian. The visitors' hair was like fire and their eyes like ice, and some of the men had faces like bears.

The Attiwandeton Indians, who once lived near the Great Lakes, said the visitors were "white people."

The Menomonie recalled that the visitors had light skin.

When presented with one of the visitors' copper artifacts, excavated in the late 18th century, a Chippewa elder responded, "White man make long ago, way back."

Today, for convenience, most people refer to the residents of Aztalan as Aztalaners. Scientists call the visitors "ArchaeoIndians." The Indians called the visitors "Marine Men." The Marine Men called themselves Tirajana.

Whoever they were, they removed more than 500,000 tons of copper from Michigan's Upper Peninsula. There were about 5,000 individual mines, each between 4 and 7 miles long, peppering three Michigan counties. If all the mines in just one of the counties were placed end to end, they would form a trench 5 miles long, 20 feet wide and 30 feet deep.

An estimated 10,000 laborers toiled there for more than a thousand years. Their technology would not be surpassed for several thousand years more. Huge stone wharves survive, supporting their reputation among the native Indians as "Marine Men." The mines themselves were outfitted with implements of every imaginable type, some of them of massive size. One of the gigantic copper ore nuggets found in one of the surviving wooden cribs weighs six tons. It is now housed at the Smithsonian Institution.

The ore was shipped south to Rock Lake, just beneath the snow line, where it was processed. Fire pits used to form the ingots have been excavated at Aztalan. We do not know where that tremendous amount of copper went after that. However, it is known that at this time—around 3000 B.C. to 1200 B.C.—Europe was enjoying its Bronze Age. Bronze is made of copper and tin. One of the great archeological mysteries of Europe has been where all the necessary copper came from. Known, workable, mixed-quality deposits in Great Britain and Spain would have been quickly exhausted. Lake Superior's shores have, and had, the only known workable virgin, native copper deposits in the world.

At the same time as the Bronze Age, at the same time as the tremendous mining in the Upper Peninsula, according to legend, Atlantis reigned supreme and was enjoying great wealth derived from its trade of precious metals, especially orichalch, throughout the known world. So abundant was their supply of orichalch that the Atlanteans built long walls of it, delineating the borders of their states. Today we call orichalch copper.

Here are three events concerning copper that occurred at the same time, in America, Europe and Atlantis: The mines in the Upper Peninsula closed precisely when Europe's Bronze Age ended; the Bronze Age was not supplanted by the Iron Age—instead, Europe stagnated. And when the Bronze Age ended, Atlantis supposedly sank.

But was Atlantis real in the first place? It probably was, but we have to realize that our image of it may differ from fact. What we know about

Aztalan State Park near Lake Mills preserves a mysterious prehistoric settlement that Indians claim was inhabited by whites and that one researcher now links to Atlantis.

the lost civilization comes from two accounts written by Plato (427 to 347 B.C.), and from possible references in the Bible.

Atlantis did not begin with Plato; he didn't just make it up. Earlier, the historian Marcellus recorded ancestral legends about Atlantis. (While the original text has been lost, commentaries on Marcellus' work have survived.) In Plato's native Greece, the story was probably part of a dim and remote folklore, with too few details for the extended descriptions Plato provided. Those details he credited to Solon, who learned the larger story in Egypt. Solon passed the legend to Dropidas, a relative of Plato, who then passed it to Critias the elder, then to Callaeschrus, then to Dropidas, then to Critias the younger, and finally to the latter's nephew, Plato.

Given the story's tortuous transmission, it is hardly surprising that Plato got Atlantis' age wrong. He placed the island's destruction in 14,000 B.C., a time in which it is hard to imagine civilization at all, let alone one of Atlantis' reported superiority. It is also difficult to believe that the Atlantis legend would have survived that long through oral history, no matter how famous it once had been.

But Plato was working from the Egyptian legend, and the Egyptians measured time differently. They were on a lunar calendar, and the Greeks were on a solar one. Corrected, the date of Atlantis' destruction moves ahead in time to 1200 B.C. Assuming that that date is rough, we can then look with more than a little interest at the geologic record. A massive volcano erupted on the island of Santorini in 1500 B.C., devastated the Mediterranean and literally buried Minoan civilization—which may have been part of Atlantis; this far back, names given millenia later by scientists mean nothing, and become frustratingly changeable.

That such a story could survive 700 or 800 years until finally recorded by Plato is fairly reasonable ... if such a place actually existed. What was it?

It was a place named for and ruled by Atlas. Spiritually, then, it was the center of the earth. And it was probably the center of commerce and government, as well.

There was a central island, at the edge of the known world. That places it somewhere outside the Mediterranean, but not necessarily far into the Atlantic. (When the Americas were discovered, however, many believed that the continents were Atlantis, and maps were labeled accordingly. Sir Francis Bacon was one of the supporters of this theory.)

Surrounding the main island were two zones of land and two zones of water, all of which were Atlantean territory. Ten kings governed the empire independently, but all were bound by a sort of common constitution and were surprisingly liberal. No single king could pronounce a death penalty without a majority vote of the other kings.

Atlantis enjoyed tremendous natural resources. The Atlanteans were expert miners, domesticators of animals, and builders. They constructed palaces, temples and docks, and joined their regions with a network of canals. They were huge consumers of copper and gold. Thanks to their expert sailors, they exploited trade opportunities throughout the known world.

And then they passed beneath the sea. The Egyptian priests who told the story to Solon made the disaster into a moral: Atlantis perished because of its "overweening pride." Similarly, many have long taken Plato's rambling account to be a parable, a myth made up to teach a lesson.

If so, Plato failed. His accounts do have symbolism, but are more like confusing and contradictory historical fact than clear prose. He teaches no lesson and there is none to be learned. So is it journalism?

Using journalism's rules, we can at least look for confirmation of the Atlanteans' actions, if not their existence. If there had been an Atlantis, and if it had been overwhelmed by a natural disaster, it follows that its survivors became refugees. Now the researcher begins to get lucky, as this is the point when recorded history begins. Stories are written down.

Dates still are murky, but in the last third of the 14th century B.C., a volcanic eruption was observed. It was a disaster of Biblical proportions—literally. This is noted in the Old Testament (Exodus 12:28). Soon after, a "People of the Sea" came to Libya, where they formed an alliance and joined in war against Egypt. The People of the Sea lost, were captured and were offered resettlement in Egypt. They accepted and flourished.

But there were other People of the Sea still searching for a new home. Some made their way to Syria, where they again formed an alliance and attacked Egypt. Again, they were captured, killed or resettled. The Sea People were scattered and incorporated into the cultures whose written histories are among the first we have.

In all, there is nothing unreasonable about the theory that Atlantis was real and that its knowledge of shipping was so advanced that its empire spanned the globe. There are enough islands, and there may have been more at the time, to provide way stations along the necessary routes. It is possible. But possibility is not proof.

But there is a funny thing about copper, or, more properly, the way it was transported in the ancient world. For shipment throughout the Mediterranean, it was cast in a very peculiar shape, which allowed it to be handled easily. The shape of the ingot was called an "ox hide," as it roughly resembled the hide of an ox. It was a square with concave sides and with legs sticking from each corner for easy handling. Bronze Age shipping vessels have been excavated in the Mediterranean, yielding many such ingots. The peculiar shape became something of an icon and was even retained for smaller ingots, used as money.

Besides the Mediterranean, ox hide ingots have been recovered from archeological sites in western Mexico.

And from Michigan's Upper Peninsula. You can see one in the Michigan State Museum in Lansing.

Plan a vacation to Aztalan. I think you'll find it interesting.

THE INDIANS' ALIEN

"I don't belong here. I dropped from above." Those are the words spoken to Chippewa Indians by a strange visitor, according to Chippewa legend.

That's why some of the Indian legends collected in 1930 by the State Historical Society of Wisconsin are of special interest to modern UFO investigators. According to the stories, Wisconsin's Indians were visited several times by "Sky-men," sometimes in strange craft.

Wisconsin historian Charles Brown, who recorded these stories, wrote intriguingly of the beliefs of the Cherokee, another Indian tribe: "There are different opinions as to the nature of the stars. Some Indians say they are balls of light, others say they are human, but most [Cherokee] people say they are living creatures covered with luminous fur or feathers."

"Luminous fur" sounds like unlikely garb for space travelers, but Brown also recorded a Chippewa tale that is surprisingly believable. Though the historian-anthropologist recorded the story decades before NASA provided us with images of real-life Sky-men and Sky-women—and 17 years before the first modern UFO sighting in 1947—this legend paints a reasonable portrait of a marooned astronaut:

"Some Indians were walking over the plains when they saw some-one sitting on the grass. It was a man. When they approached, he halt-ed them by raising his hand.

"He said, 'I don't belong here. I dropped from above.' They wished to take him home with them. He told them to go home and clean the place where he was to stay. Then he would return with them. After they had done this, they came back for him. He was a nice-looking man, clean and shining bright. He stayed with them.

"Every day at sundown, he watched the sky. In a clear voice he said, 'Something will come down, I will go up.' He said that he had been running in the sky. There was an open place, he couldn't stop running, so he dropped through.

"One day in the afternoon he said, 'Now it's coming.' Everyone looked up but they could see nothing for a long time. The man who had kept Sky-man at his home could see better than the others. He saw a brilliant star shining way up in the sky. The other Indians did-n't see it until it came near the ground. They had never seen anything nicer in the world.

"Two men got hold of it and pulled it down. Sky-man got into it. Then it rose and he was gone. They had tried to get him to stay but he said that he must go.

"He is up there yet. You can see him on clear nights."

Was Sky-man "clean and shining" because he wore a silvery pres-sure-suit? If the legend is true, it's possible that the visitor insisted on clean quarters for fear of encountering human viruses against which he had no resistance.

Did Sky-man ever come back to thank his Indian rescuers? Per-haps. If so, he passed unrecognized, his Indian hosts displaced by a less hospitable civilization.

UFOs COME FROM ...
BARABOO?

C ould it be that UFOS do not come from other worlds, but from ... Wisconsin?

At the close of the 19th century, thousands of people saw strange things in the sky, attributing them sometimes to aliens but more often to secretive inventors, among them Wisconsin's own Ringling brothers of circus fame. And, oddly enough, there's some period testimony to back up the latter theory.

Sightings of a mystery airship began in late April 1896 in California and gradually spread east, ending—perhaps significantly—in Madison, not far from Baraboo, winter quarters for the Ringling Bros. Circus.

"In major cities like Sacramento, Omaha and Chicago, thousands rushed into the streets or clambered to rooftops to view the vessel as it passed," wrote Daniel Cohen in his history of the phenomena, *The Great Airship Mystery*.

People have seen strange things in the sky since Biblical times, coming up with explanations that fit their cultures, technologies and theologies. It wasn't until after World War II that extraterrestrials were given the nod. Just 50 years before that, hovering cigar-shaped objects were believed to be manmade inventions, something like dirigibles. But while dirigible technology was fairly advanced in 1896—an experimental craft flew successfully in France in 1882—a practical, maneuverable airship was not yet on the scene. Historically, the 1896 sightings are impossible to explain in terms of dirigibles.

There were other big balloons around, however, and circuses featured balloon ascensions as attractions. "From 1871 through about 1894, balloon feats rivaled the free street parade as a street attraction," wrote Bob Parkinson in the circus magazine, *The Bandwagon*, in 1961.

While the round, hydrogen-filled balloons of the circuses could not account for the swift comings and goings of the mystery airship, circuses were working on better craft. By 1905, Pawnee Bill's Wild West Show featured a self-propelled airship. Had the Ringlings been experimenting earlier?

One of the first mystery airship sightings occurred on the night of Nov. 22, 1896, in Sacramento. Walter Mallory, a deputy sheriff, described it as "a strong white light" with a dark body immediately over it. At 1 p.m. the airship was sighted in Tacoma, Wash. A mere half hour later it was seen in San Jose, Calif., 750 miles away. The next evening it was in Los Angeles. Sightings continued all over the state.

William Randolph Hearst's *San Francisco Examiner* initially ignored the excitement, but at last announced on Nov. 28, "The biggest problem of the age has been solved. Man has won his hardest battle with nature. A successful airship has been built."

On Feb. 2, 1897, the airship appeared in Hastings, Neb. Three days later it was 40 miles south, in Invale, Neb. On March 27 it was in Topeka, Kan., where it was seen by several hundred people, including the state's governor, who said, "I don't know what the whole thing is, but I hope it may yet solve the railroad problem." (Kansas was then in the grip of the rail trust.)

On April 4, it was in Wisconsin, but then it backtracked, and on April 10 it was in Keokuk, Iowa. In Waterloo, the airship appeared to have crashed, but the wreckage viewed by hundreds turned out to be a hoax. Sightings continued in Texas, Arkansas, Missouri, Wisconsin and Illinois.

Newspapers in Chicago tracked the airship and predicted its speed. They announced that it would arrive around April 9, and it did. On that day it was seen by 500 people in Evanston, Ill. It stayed in the area three days, long enough to be photographed. Sadly, the photo has been lost, though hand-drawn copies survive.

The mystery airship had a rugged schedule, suggesting either incredible speed or the presence of a whole fleet. It flew over these Wisconsin communities on the following dates: Darlington on April 4; Wausau on April 8; Fort Atkinson and Rice Lake on April 9; Chilton, Fond du Lac, Manitowoc and Marshfield on April 10; Appleton, Cumberland, Delavan, Eau Claire, Kenosha, Madison, Merrillan, Milwaukee, Rio and Ripon (where 180 people saw it) on April 11; Appleton, Hayward, Lodi and Superior on April 12; Brodhead, Clayton, Durand and Spooner on April 13; Darien and Turtle Lake on April 14; Lake Mills on April 22.

On the night of April 11, "every adult citizen of Milwaukee, in common with the adult population of the great Northwest, swept the 'infinite meadow of heaven' ... in search for the mysterious airship," reported the *Milwaukee Sentinal*. A group at the corner of North Broadway Street and East Kilbourn Avenue saw it—or thought they did. Harry E. Moore, stationkeeper at the Central Police Station, said, "It was too large for a star—about as big as four ordinary stars. And besides this, it bobbed up and down, skipped off southward."

The newspaper noted that "the colors, red, white and green, which it exhibited, were too distinct, many thought, to have been the result of atmospheric refraction."

In Appleton, on the next night, "the light was no larger than a large star, but changed color from red to a piercing white, more closely resembling an electric searchlight at several miles distance," again according to the *Sentinal*. "What was even more peculiar, the 'airship' seemed to bob up and down with at times a lateral motion. When still some degrees above the horizon, it disappeared, reappearing again in an instant, and finally became invisible."

On April 11, the airship appeared over Madison, where several witnesses saw the bright lights of a cigar-shaped object. It returned to Madison on April 14, launching a war of words between Madison and Milwaukee journalists.

Some Madisonians called the university's Washburn Observatory, where astronomer G.C. Comstock refused to take the reports seriously; he said the airship could be the planet Jupiter or Venus. The *Sentinal*, deriding the professor, reported that the planets "have color decorations and might possibly be taken for an airship, or even a house and lot."

The Madison papers scoffed at it all, reporting that one resident with unusually good eyesight said the object had a double hull, like a catamaran. He also said that a name was written on one side: "Star Tickler." And "a lady who was brought up with the Indians and has very sharp hearing, says she caught a glimpse of a face laughing as if it would split and heard a voice say, 'Has the sucker fishing begun down there yet?' "

Madison's *Wisconsin State Journal* reported that the object "wavered up and down just as the boats of the Aerial Rapid Transport line might be expected to do." Funny stuff—and familiar stuff to ufologists who have long puzzled over the wobbling "falling-leaf" motion so often associated with modern saucer sightings. And the paper's own skepticism shows that the phenomena, if a hoax, at least wasn't a press-sponsored hoax.

Then, on April 20, the airship largely vanished. After a few appearances in Indiana, its eastward trip stopped.

What had happened?

For one thing, a practical explanation had finally been put forward. One of the more believable explanations came when a Madison newspaper pointed out that the airship's appearance in Chicago occurred "almost simultaneously with the advent to that city of the Ringlings." One of the brothers was even observed transporting "large and mysterious bundles" from the circus grounds.

A reporter sent to Baraboo found that residents there were "of the opinion that the airship was a succession of balloons or something of the kind, which were aimed to prey upon the curiosity of an incredulous public to the end that shining half dollars would pour into the big wagons where tickets for the big show are sold."

On April 15, the *Chicago Times-Herald* stated that the airship was definitely the product of the Ringlings' Baraboo workshops, where it was still being tested and perfected. The article said that the airship was based on a model created by a New York inventor, built by a man named Carr and further developed by the Ringlings.

The Ringling brothers denied it, and so does a leading circus historian today.

"I've never heard of any dirigible experiments with the Ringling show," said Fred Dahlinger Jr., director of the circus library and research center at Baraboo's Circus World Museum, housed in the very same workshops where the airship was allegedly created. "I really would find it hard to believe that any show at that time would do anything with dirigibles," he told me.

Still, the airship visited Baraboo on April 11 and 13, and when it put in its last appearance, more than a decade later, it was again in the Ringlings' back yard, Madison. On Sept. 10, 1910, east-side residents of the capital city looked into the sky and saw "a ship approaching from the north, headed south across Lake Mendota," said the *Wisconsin State Journal*. Mrs. Nils Starck, Mrs. Mary Malaney and the Joe Helmus family said it began "slowing down, descending, hovering, as if seeking a place to land, then flying off to the southwest."

It was never seen again. At least, a strange object in the sky was never again described as a Victorian "airship."

Whatever it was, whether the Ringlings constructed it or not, the airship had created a spectacle on a mammoth stage, thrilling thousands from California to Indiana. Truly, it was the greatest show on Earth—or, more accurately, above it. And the performance may continue yet.

CHASED BY A SAUCER IN STOUGHTON

Did a damaged flying saucer make an emergency landing in Stoughton in 1968?

At 7 p.m. Sunday, Jan. 21, Shirley Kortte and Mrs. W.W. Knipfer were driving along Interstate 90 near Janesville. In the back seat were their daughters, Judy Kortte and Ida and Stephanie Knipfer.

"We had just come from Janesville," Kortte told me. "The girls were in a dance recital." Now they were asleep, except for one girl who looked out and saw a UFO.

As the witnesses approached the County N interchange near Stoughton, they stopped, "because I was driving and very scared," Shirley Kortte said. The large, round, dark-gray object then appeared to drop sparks and flaming debris—a rare but not unknown UFO behavior. The object was about the size of a hot-air balloon, and was about as far away as "the top of a barn" might be when observed from a barnyard. The UFO came so close that it seemed as if it might even strike the car. "You could almost see the bottom of it," Kortte said. "Then, of course, these sparks came out of it, so you couldn't see real clear. By this time we had some screaming girls."

Knipfer said that the object continued its pursuit even as she pulled into the driveway of her home, near the east shore of Lake Kegonsa. "I didn't quite get in the driveway, I was shaking so."

The object then crossed the Yahara River to the east, and seemed to land north of the Oscar Berge farm. Sheriff's deputy Robert Shaffer was already on hand. With three more witnesses—apparently neighboring youths—he, too, watched the object disappear from view. Shaffer's search for additional witnesses was unsuccessful.

Kortte remembers that someone went to the Berge farm and did see something on the ground there. More than that, no one knows. However, I believe that physical evidence was recovered, as we shall see in a later chapter.

Disturbing? Certainly. And add to that the testimony of 30 others, including four Freeport, Ill., police officers and three Stephenson County, Ill., sheriff's deputies who saw a similar UFO on Nov. 9, 1967, just two months earlier. Two men reported that while they drove on Highway 20 very early that day they were followed for 28 miles by a bright object that was flying 500 to 1,000 feet above the ground. The Associated Press reported that Freeport police were alerted, and after the responding officers had driven just three miles, they also saw the highway gremlin. They kept it under observation from 4:15 to 6:30 a.m. The county sheriff's deputies watched, too—from their office. At Freeport Memorial Hospital, 25 patients and staff also observed the object.

TAKE ME TO YOUR LEADER: MADISON UFOs

In Wisconsin, the above request would direct the curious interstellar tourist to Madison, the state capital. The city falls within a belt of UFO sightings, the state's south-central flying saucer "window."

Nancy Goff, age 13, landed in the newspapers by being the first to report a Madison UFO. On the night of July 7, 1947, she was sitting on the porch of her family's home, at 1042 Williamson St. Around 10:30 p.m. she saw something that looked like "a plate upside-down."

"I saw a light flash on the ground," she told reporters. "When I looked in the sky I saw a flying disc. It kept turning different colors and was moving very fast but disappeared in a little while."

That same night, Richard Y. Schulkin, 719 Mound St., saw "some sort of gliding missile, of convex shape," flying over south Madison. Schulkin said the object was traveling rapidly and was heading south. He thought it was silver in color, and possibly made of aluminum.

The next sighting was of an unusual light on April 16, 1952. The Air Force investigated this sighting of a nocturnal light but turned up no useful information. It also investigated a sighting made at 5:45 p.m. on Dec. 9, 1952: Capt. Bridges and 1st Lt. Johnson were flying over Madison in an Air Force T-33 trainer when they saw four bright lights moving in diamond formation at 450 mph. The Air Force listed the 10-minute encounter as an unknown. Another brush with the Air Force came on Aug. 16, 1966, when a UFO was seen on radar at Madison's Truax Field.

Shortly before 8:30 p.m. on Feb. 5, 1968, Elvi Sanchez and her 15-year-old daughter, Gloria, saw a light in the sky north of their home, at 4810 South Hill Drive. They told police that the light silently passed their house at a high rate of speed, then stopped in midair about a block away. It stayed there a few minutes, hovering about 50 feet above the ground. The UFO focused a large beam of light on the ground, then disappeared. The women first thought they might have seen an airplane, but then realized that they had heard no engine during the incident.

Between 6 and 6:30 p.m. on Sept. 8, 1971, Mrs. A. Georgeson looked up on her way to a Madison bowling alley, and on the horizon saw a "vapor trail," such as those sometimes left by jet aircraft. The trail was short and well-defined, and it did not grow, as would a true vapor trail. As Georgeson watched, she decided that what she was looking at was actually a bright, cigar-shaped UFO.

Between 8:30 and 9:30 p.m. that same day, Martin Verhoven and his wife, Chris, were traveling north on Highway 14, approaching Madison's Beltline Highway, when they noticed a colored light in the sky to the west. The light moved erratically—starting and stopping, moving up and down—but in general followed the Beltline west. It was so unusual that they pulled over to watch it. As the light moved, it changed from orange to red, but when it stopped it was silver-white. The sighting lasted about 15 minutes.

At 10 p.m. that night, four women were driving along the 5700 block of Pheasant Hill Road when they saw what they at first thought was an airplane traveling "on a strange angle." The driver later said that the red box-shaped or triangle-shaped object had three sets of lights, from "wingtip to wingtip and on the tail." Along each side of the 40-foot UFO were 10 or so lights. It was about as tall as the steeple of nearby St. Stephen's Church. After a single minute, the object flew northwest.

Three days later, Mrs. Georgeson, who had made the initial sighting in this small UFO wave, became the sort of witness that investigators traditionally fear most: a "repeater." (Given the unlikely nature of a UFO report in the first place, the odds that a single witness will experience more than one sighting are poor indeed. This bias against repeaters has been relaxed, however, in light of the recent spate of reports of abductions, which typically occur many times over the abductee's lifetime.)

At any rate, during her second observation, Georgeson was accompanied by her two children. The three witnesses were driving south on Park Street when they spotted a UFO. It hovered for about 10 minutes over south Madison. The object was cigar-shaped, more blunt on one end than the other, and seemed to pivot in the sky. It was the size of a quarter or half-dollar held at arm's length. The family got on the Beltline and headed west, and as they approached Nakoma Road they believed the object was banking or "tipping." Another UFO was observed the same day by David Joranson, over Lake Monona.

On March 14, 1975, Charles Larson said he and his wife used binoculars to watch a strange object near their home on Old Sauk Road. They observed the object for about half an hour, beginning at 9 p.m. Larson and his wife said the object looked like "two plates held together, with one inverted over the other," with a row of lights along the edge. It moved rapidly in several directions and then headed west, toward Cross Plains. The object was also observed by their neighbor, Lawrence Wollangk, a University of Wisconsin researcher, who said it "was no star."

Probably the most reliable sighting to occur in Madison was on the night of May 3, 1975. Among the six or seven witnesses were two Madison police officers, who waited 10 days before filing a written report of what they believed they had seen.

The UFO was first spotted by workers at a gas station on Odana Road near Whitney Way. They watched the oval-shaped object for more than an hour as it hovered near the WKOW-TV towers at Tokay Boulevard. "It wasn't twinkling like a star," said Scott Bianco, a 19-year-old employed at the station. He and a friend, Carol Wecklem, and at least two other employees watched the object with police officers Luis Yudice and Steven Cardarella. The officers later reported that they did "observe the object, which seemed to gradually gain brightness."

The object disappeared several times, reappeared with increased brightness, then finally disappeared for good. Cardarella told me, "I just didn't know what it was at the time." But he didn't think it was reflected light from a helicopter or a weather balloon.

On July 31, 1976, Mary A. Tall and her mother, Isabel T. Frast, of

5201 Dorsett Drive, saw a very large, bright-blue, fast-moving object in the sky, at around 2:30 p.m. "My mother saw it first," said Tall. "I didn't believe her." Then Tall saw it, too, but only briefly: "I wasn't too eager to go outside and find out what that thing was."

At 7 p.m. on Nov. 13, 1979, Ms. Billy Sager, Raymond Warner and at least four others saw a nocturnal light streak across the sky over Madison's east side.

An anonymous woman told the *Madison Press Connection* newspaper that she and her two children had seen a UFO on the city's west side on Jan. 31, 1979.

In 1985 something hovered over Madison streets that later observers might call "stealth" aircraft. But this was years before the existence of the Air Force's radar-invisible flying-wing aircraft was made public. At 11 p.m. on Nov. 19, a woman was driving near the East Madison Baptist Church on Milwaukee Street. The only illumination came from her car's headlights, a single streetlight and three lights above a row of trees next to the church. The last three lights looked unusual to the woman, the sister of a friend of a reporter at the *Wisconsin State Journal*. She later told the journalist her story, though she asked to remain unidentified in the article.

The lights appeared to be those of a helicopter descending toward a house on the north side of the street. It came within 10 feet of the road. "I was curious, of course, because if the craft continued on its present course it would crash into the house," the woman said. "So I decided to pull over to the curb, never taking my eyes off the lights."

The row of lights made a sharp and graceful 90-degree turn just short of the curb. "Now moving towards me, it rises slightly in the middle of the block," the woman said, reliving her thoughts at the time in the present tense. "Ascending straight up, several feet in front of my car, the craft avoids hitting the power lines."

As the object rose, the streetlight illuminated it.

"The craft is triangular, about 12 feet in length and black," she said. "A light shines from the narrow nose. The body gradually widens but remains trim—too trim for a person to be comfortably seated. A wide silver streak extends from the nose to the tail. The view is partially obstructed by a light."

No wings, propellers, no engines of any sort were visible. Whatever it was, it was silent. It swept north, hovering 12 to 15 feet above a house. The rear of the object was about half the width of the roof.

"Two white lights flank the rear, and a small red light is near the light on the right," the woman said. "Rectangular white lights flash on near the top and are blinking in rapid succession. The lights are moving in a seemingly circular motion. The bottom is slightly convex."

She was frightened. She left and called the police. Sgt. Ray Warner responded. "She was real rational," he said. "She definitely saw something. I don't know what, but she saw something." Radar at the Dane County Regional Airport was not operating at the time, and the object's low altitude would have hidden it from radar screens anyway.

Three days later, at about 5 p.m. on Nov. 22, a state employee was driving on County CV near Chase Lumber, when he saw three similar lights in the sky. They were hovering 20 to 30 feet above a farmhouse. At first he thought he was seeing a helicopter.

"Then I realized I didn't know what it was," he said. The object was roughly triangular with a sloping bottom, and moved silently. When the man stopped and got out of his car to investigate, the object left.

At 2 a.m. May 12, 1995, University of Wisconsin students observed a strange "bootlike" object in the sky over Lake Mendota. I assume that this is similar to reports of delta-wing or triangle-shaped craft, which appear to be displacing the classic saucer shape as the century closes.

At 10:30 p.m. on Oct. 14, 1995, a family of four telephoned 911 to report a very bright "pointed oval object." When the light dimmed, "spikes sticking out" became apparent.

At 10 p.m. on Jan. 20, 1996, an anonymous Madisonian told the Seattle-based UFO Information Center, (s)he had seen a cigar-shaped craft with "eight dim blue and red lights" along its length.

Of all Madison's sightings, the most dramatic occurred on Sept. 1, 1970. It was 10:10 p.m. Denise Fritz and Mike Butler were out in a boat on Lake Monona when they looked up and saw a "lighted object" heading toward the water. They first thought it was a plane in trouble.

"It looked like it was going to crash," Fritz said. "We joked about flying saucers, but we still assumed it was a plane." They changed their minds when they saw the object hover between 50 and 100 feet above some trees near a boat landing on Winnequah Road.

"It looked like it was an oval," said Fritz, "but I couldn't focus on it well enough to make out the whole shape. I don't know what it was, but I've never seen anything like it."

Fritz and Butler had stopped their motor, but they could hear no sound from the object. Suddenly, the object beamed two lights at the boat. The couple started the motor again and began to leave. The object followed them.

"When we swerved to the left, the lights turned to the left, too," said Fritz. "When we tuned right, the lights turned right. By this time we were pretty scared."

At the same time, the UFO was seen by four Monona women who wouldn't give their names to reporters. (Said one, "People will think I'm some kind of nut.")

The women were riding in a car and had almost reached the corner of Bridge Road and Panther Trail when they saw something in the sky to the northeast. "It seemed at first that it might be a low-flying plane," one woman said, "but it had a lot of lights on."

Fritz and Butler, meanwhile, were scrambling to escape.

"We went back to the pier as fast as we could, and it—the lights—followed us," said Fritz. "We didn't even tie up the boat. We ran right into the house. I was shaking and crying for about two hours, I was so scared."

Back at the intersection of Bridge and Panther, the four women got out of their car for a better look. Like Fritz, they said they had a hard time focusing their eyes on the object. "We couldn't make out a shape," one said. "I don't believe in flying saucers or that sort of thing, but I don't understand this, because whatever this thing was, it made no sound at all."

The women watched as the object flew away. For them, the incident was over. For Fritz and Butler, it was to continue for some time.

"I have no doubt that it was something not from around here," Fritz told me. "For a long time we didn't go out in the boat at night. I have chills about it even now."

AMERICA'S SAUCERLAND
A Complete List of
Wisconsin UFO Reports

I have taken tremendous pains to compile what I believe is the most complete list of Wisconsin UFO reports ever made. Some are brief, some are boring; all are unexplained.

A word about the terminology: The study of UFOs, casually referred to as "ufology," does have a rudimentary science to it, thanks in large part to the efforts of two leaders in the field, computer scientist Jacques Vallee and astronomer J. Allen Hynek. Both men created classification systems for the cursory discussion of what previously had been summarized only as flying saucers or flying discs. For our purposes, I am using only Hynek's systems.

"UFO," meaning unidentified flying object, originally was a euphemism and an acronym coined by the U.S. Air Force; it was applied to objects before they were studied, as in, "the UFO turned out to be a weather balloon." If, after study, the sighting still defied description, the Air Force dropped the UFO label and called it an "unknown."

Private ufologists, however, tend to reserve the term "UFO" for objects that survive scrutiny, as in "the bright, shining object was not

Venus but a UFO." In the following listings of UFOs, I use the term only in the sense that the object was unidentified to the witness; it may be that many of the reports have more conventional explanations. Where the cases have survived Air Force scrutiny, I have noted that fact; the vast majority of these reports were not, however, reported to the Air Force in the first place. (And since 1969 the Air Force has refused to examine civilian reports. Rather strict regulations still require reports be made of UFOs by military personnel, within military channels.)

Hynek's two classification systems have gained a lot of currency in popular culture, without a lot of understanding. The first describes the object's appearance:

- Nocturnal light. By far the most common sort of sighting, nocturnal light can look like a star or a planet, which is often what it turns out to be. It can also occur in the morning and evening, in which cases Venus is a very likely suspect.
- Daylight disc. This is our old friend the flying saucer, which in reality (well, the reality of UFOs, at least) comes in a bewildering variety of shapes and sizes; boomerang, triangle, cross—you name it, someone sometime has seen it. As Hynek points out, distant daylight discs may account for nocturnal lights, and it is also true that during the day some UFOs appear to simply be fast-moving points of light. Strangely, the objects that are most often reported change shape over time, with fair consistency. It's almost as if new makes and models come out and are bought by style-conscious aliens; this, in fact, has been the conclusion of some Air Force personnel. These days, triangular craft are reported with greater and greater frequency, replacing the classic domed platter.
- Radar sighting. UFOs on radar screens are not as rare as you might think, although these days they are quite a bit more rare than they previously were since civilian airport radars no longer "paint" all airborne objects and return the signals. Instead, they look for the radar transponders aboard aircraft. But even earlier in aviation history, a radar return did not provide certain knowledge of a UFO, as temperature inversions and other atmospheric peculiarities could give a false return. Radar-visual sightings, on the other hand, with radar returns and eyewitness

observation, are hard to argue against.

Hynek's second and better-known classification system ordered the proximity and behavior of the observed UFO, relative to the witness:

- Close encounter of the first kind. For a sighting to be classified as such, the object must be less than a couple hundred feet away. As opposed to seeing a distant, disc-shaped light, in this case, one sees some details and perceives depth. For this reason, stars, planes, etc., are almost certainly ruled out.
- Close encounter of the second kind. In this situation, the UFO interacts with the viewer or environment. It follows our car, avoids intercepting aircraft, changes course in a logical manner. Landing marks may be made, grass may be charred, or debris may fall from the object—like the so-called gossamer threads of "angel hair" that, theoretically, are made of ionized air sleeting off an electromagnetic field surrounding the object. The skeptics' constant call for hard evidence begins to be answered here; the Chicago-based Center for UFO Studies has logged more than 800 of these physical trace cases.
- Close encounter of the third kind. Entities are observed, and we may now safely call the objects "craft," for they are certainly occupied. Everything from can-sized robots to Scandinavian humans in ski suits have been seen in close encounters of the third kind. Strangely, there have been very few bizarre monsters—no oily tentacles, no bubbling, sucking masses of flesh, dripping with viscous slime, as in War of the Worlds. These days, as you probably know, the most common tourist to our solar system is the "gray," a slim, naked lad with no genitalia, no nose, a swollen head and wrap-around eyes.

Since Hynek's death, another rank has been added, close encounters of the fourth kind, encompassing the abduction phenomena.

UFOs are incredibly common in Wisconsin. One U.S. Air Force summary shows that—with the exception of a section of New Mexico—the north-central region of the country has the largest number of unexplained sightings. Of the states in the north-central region, Wisconsin has the most.

I apologize here for the sketchiness of some of the listings. I have given extended descriptions for unusually novel sightings. In some cases, I have tried unsuccessfully to find more material on certain sightings, and have only the information given here. I have not included reports that are clearly bogus, or reports that I believe have been reasonably explained.

To my mind, the strongest evidence supporting the reality of UFOs comes, simply, from the large number of reports. Can all of the following witnesses have been wrong? Could at least one of them have been right? It's for that reason that I have chosen to emphasize the vast number of reports rather than just those I have been able to study in depth. Madison reports, because of their great number, are listed in a separate chapter. When reports cluster within a few days and around a single location, I have combined the reports in a single listing.

Here they are:

ADAMS, NOVEMBER 1964: Two parents and their three sons experienced a close encounter of the second kind.

ALGOMA , OCTOBER 1951: Nocturnal light, observed by Mark Kopecky.

AMERY, OCT. 6, 1979, 7:30 P.M.: A man, 66, and wife, 51, observed a nocturnal light.

ANTIGO, NOV. 17, 1974: Close encounter of the third kind.

ANTIGO, 11:22 TO 11:42 P.M., OCT. 30, 1980: Three women called the sheriff's department and reported a nocturnal light.

APOSTLE ISLANDS, JULY 29, 1978, 2:40 A.M.: The crew of a Coast Guard ship observed a nocturnal light.

APPLETON, SEPT. 26, 1972: Close encounter of the first kind, four miles west of the city.

APPLETON, AUG. 2, 1975: Close encounter of the first kind.

APPLETON, JAN. 26, 1969: Close encounter of the second kind.

APPLETON, MARCH 22, 1967: Frank Goddard observed a nocturnal light.

ASHLAND, MARCH 13, 1975: Authorities in four northern counties reported UFO sightings. (This event is treated at length in a separate chapter.) The reports were followed one night later by a sighting in nearby Mellen and in south-central Wisconsin.

ASHLAND, SEPT. 4, 1979, 8:15 P.M.: Two boys, ages 13 and 14, had a close encounter of the first kind.

AUBURNDALE, OCT. 19, 1977: Cliff Borden, news director of WFHR-AM radio in Wisconsin Rapids, and Terry Stake, the station's sports director, saw a "bright, white light" while duck hunting at Mead Wildlife Area, seven miles northeast of town. The two were leaving the marsh at around 7 p.m. Borden, 47, told the Associated Press, "He and I saw precisely the same thing. We were walking east on a dike. The thing was directly in front of us." The light flashed at times, like "a very intense strobe light," alternately hovering and traveling an erratic path, eventually moving out of sight to the east. When the object was stationary it looked "like you might observe a distant plane," Borden said. But then "it would go up and down and to the side like a helicopter ... but it was too high for a helicopter." Similar reports were made the same night in Neillsville, west of Auburndale, in Clark County.

BALDWIN, OCT. 20, 1979: Eight miles south of town Scott Sieracki observed a nocturnal light; possible landing traces were found.

BALSAM LAKE, OCT. 25, 1979, 6:30 A.M.: Five miles east of town, Richard Breault and his wife experienced a close encounter of the first kind.

BARABOO AND SOUTH-CENTRAL WISCONSIN, SEPT. 22, 1974: At least six Wisconsin state troopers and one state game warden reported seeing "a large object in the sky with red, green and blue flashing lights." A state patrol spokesperson said that troopers Joe Noll and Walter Dunford sighted the object shortly before 4 a.m., apparently near Sparta. It was stationary at first, then moved slowly away. At the same time troopers in Madison observed what they believed to be the same object. From their vantage point, they said the object appeared to be over the Baraboo area. Madison's Truax Field reported no aircraft in the area at the time.

BARRON, SUMMER 1934: Daylight disc observed.

BAYFIELD COUNTY, NOV. 21, 1978: County deputies observed nocturnal lights. They were also observed by Tom Adams, Jack Dixon and Dan Leman, who photographed them.

BAYFIELD, SEPT. 15, 1975: Daylight disc observed by Gardner Hadland.

BEAVER BROOK (WASHBURN COUNTY), AUG. 26, 1978: Possible landing marks were discovered on the property of Charles Larson.

BEAVER DAM, MAY 8, 1966: John Beers told police that he and a friend were traveling south on County G, south of the city, when they saw blinking white and green lights pacing his car, flying above telephone poles next to the road. He turned right at Lipsic, and the object followed the car to Highway 151, then to Columbus, where it headed toward Portage.

BELOIT, NOV. 23, 1960: Nocturnal light seen on the Dougan Farm, on Colley Road.

BELOIT, JUNE 26, 1962: Nocturnal light observed by Jack Reiley on the 1700 block of Arlington Avenue.

BELOIT, FEB. 13, 1969: Nocturnal light observed by Gene Brazdon.

BIRCHWOOD, FEB. 18, 1982: Nocturnal light observed by two witnesses.

BLACK EARTH AND SURROUNDING AREA, AUG. 2, 1985: Around 9:45 p.m., 10 people, in a region that spreads from Cross Plains to Blue Mounds, saw a UFO moving slowly eastward. It was white, brighter than a star and, according to one witness, projected a beam of light that "moved back and forth like a searchlight." This is a recurring feature in Wisconsin sightings and globally is sometimes reported to be a precursor to abductions. At about the same time, 21 witnesses in six states, from Iowa to Ohio, made similar sightings, according to the Seattle-based National UFO Reporting Center. The first Wisconsinite to report the object was Rogers Keene, a teacher at Wisconsin Heights Junior High School. He was walking his dog around his rural home, five miles north of Black Earth, when he saw the slowly moving light. At first it was due south, in the direction of Black Earth, at about 75 degrees above the horizon. Keene said that the object was the size of his thumb when his arm was stretched away from his body. It was in view for two minutes, during which it swept a beam back and forth. It stopped in the southeast and descended slowly in a zig-zag pattern until it was only 20 degrees above the horizon. The light then "disappeared into a pinpoint," according to Keene, and then disappeared completely. The National Weather Service and Madison's Truax Field reported that the object did not appear on radar.

BLACK RIVER FALLS, MARCH 14, 1966: Nocturnal light observed.

BLANCHARDVILLE, SEPT. 5, 1981: Possible landing traces found by Robert Johnson.

BRILLION, DEC. 13, 1980, 5:15 A.M.: Alan and Barbara Blum observed a "big, white light ... [with] red and green flashing lights, and it didn't move."

BROOKFIELD, AUG. 13, 1978, 11:20 P.M.: A nocturnal light was observed on North Brookfield Road by two Brookfield police officers and another witness.

BROOKFIELD, OCT. 31, 1978, 7 P.M.: Nocturnal light observed.

BROWNTOWN, APRIL 20, 1969: Robert Phillips had a close encounter of the first kind, one mile west of town on Highway 11.

BURLINGTON, JULY 6, 1947: Gordon Nielson observed a nocturnal light southwest of town.

BURLINGTON, AUGUST 1948: M.L. Amoreaux observed a nocturnal light.

BURLINGTON, SEPT. 7, 1956: Daylight disc.

BURLINGTON, AUG. 8, 1978: Pat Nelson and Dean Willich observed nocturnal lights over Henry Street.

CAMERON, AUG. 16, 1966: Close encounter of the second kind, east of town.

CECIL, SEPT. 29, 1972: Nocturnal light observed by R.W. Pederson.

CHILI (CLARK COUNTY), OCT. 20, 1972, 4:10 A.M.: Verlyn Rollins saw a red and white UFO going up and down in the air east of Chili Corners.

CHIPPEWA FALLS, SUMMER 1954: Leon L. Deming observed a daylight disc.

CHIPPEWA FALLS, DEC. 28, 1954: Close encounter of the second kind.

CHIPPEWA FALLS, 1965: Close encounter of the second kind.

CHIPPEWA FALLS, AUG. 11, 1968: Jean Perry observed a nocturnal light and photographed it.

CHIPPEWA FALLS, JAN. 26, 1975: Kevin Guibord observed a nocturnal light.

CLAYTON, OCT. 13, 1979, 10 P.M.: Pam Overburg and a coworker observed a UFO.

CLINTONVILLE, SEPT. 26, 1972: Nocturnal light.

COCHRANE, APRIL 4, 1968: Close encounter of the second kind, on Highway 35.

COLFAX, APRIL 19, 1978: UFO photographed.

COLUMBUS, JUNE 18, 1952, 9 A.M.: R.A. Finger observed a crescent-shaped object hover for several seconds, then speed away. The sighting was investigated by the Air Force, which listed it as unknown.

COLUMBUS, JUNE 5, 1975: Tom Heiman and Charlotte Blob, UFO authorities who were traveling from Appleton to Madison to appear on a radio talk show, spotted three UFOs. The first sighting occurred between 9:30 and 9:50 a.m. The object was a few miles north of Columbus, and was headed north/northeast. The second object spotted was just south of town. "It was a very bright object with a long trail. It came down and split apart like a booster rocket from straight overhead, arching down southwest," Heiman said. The third UFO was spotted at 10:10 p.m., and was headed from southwest to northeast.

COON VALLEY, AUG. 13, 1995, 11:10 P.M.: A couple saw a "bright, blue, flickering light" through the cloud cover. They said it was definitely moving.

CROSS PLAINS, SEPT. 29, 1978, 8:15 P.M.: Twelve-year-olds Joel Ward and Mike Dresen observed a UFO.

CUDAHY, JULY 8, 1947: Nocturnal light observed.

CUDAHY, AUG. 25, 1985, 6:15 P.M.: A resident stopped into the offices of the Cudahy and St. Francis *Advisor Press* to report that he had seen a UFO flying about 20 feet over the trees. "It was revolving and making all sorts of reflections," he said. "There was a fellow in the next block who saw it, too. He followed it as it turned the corner about a block away."

CUMBERLAND, MARCH 22, 1978: Jim Nystrom observed a nocturnal light five miles west of town, on Highway 48.

CUMBERLAND, JAN. 19, 1980: On this night, odd lights in the sky were observed throughout the area by many different parties, including Dorie and Sarah Zahs, Percy and Betty Riley, the Sundvall family, Craig and Carolyn Greener, Mr. and Mrs. Harold Scharmers, Fred Miller, Herb Schweitzer, Bob and Joyce Nesvold and Bob and Dorothy Thorp. The Air Force later said the lights were from aircraft training flights.

DARLINGTON, JUNE 1, 1953: Glen Winslow observed a nocturnal light.

DELAFIELD, MARCH 22, 1967: Carl Rohde observed a nocturnal light near Lapham Peak.

DELAVAN, JAN. 14, 1978: Nocturnal light observed.

DENMARK, FEB. 2, 1995, 7:15 P.M.: Many people saw a strange craft streaking across the night sky. The UFO was blue and cone-shaped; its leading edge had a radiant red hue and its trailing edge had a radiant green hue. It descended quickly and hovered. In pursuit were observed four to five military-type jets; this is a not uncommon theme of 1950s sightings, seldom reported today. One woman and her two children watched the object for 75 minutes. Similar sightings—with accompanying aircraft—were reported 45 minutes later in Eastport, Mich., and 50 minutes later in Traverse City, Mich. The Traverse City witness reported the sighting to the USAF Recovery Coordination Center at Langley Air Force Base, in Virginia. The Air Force forwarded the report to the private National UFO Reporting Center.

DODGEVILLE, 1947: Eleven men watched an "undescribed" object fly in counterclockwise circles for an hour. The sighting was investigated by the Air Force, which listed it as an unknown.

DOOR COUNTY, AUG. 17, 1975, 5:10 A.M.: Dean T. Anderson saw a daylight disc at Peninsula State Park. He saw it, or an object like it, at the park again at 3:30 a.m. on July 11, 1976, when he experienced a close encounter of the third kind. He saw it yet again in the park, at 3:45 a.m. on July 22, 1976, but this time the experience was a close encounter of the first kind, though Anderson reported suffering physiological effects as a result. At 4 a.m. on Aug. 16, 1976, he had the good fortune to visit the park, have another sighting, and actually meet one of the UFO's occupants. Anderson said the alien was from Mars and its name was Muton. At 4:15 a.m. on Aug. 23, 1976, Anderson's park visitors were Sunar, a man, and Treena, a woman, both from Jupiter. On Aug. 28, 1976, Anderson saw nine UFOs over the park. I do not have a lot of confidence in Mr. Anderson.

DRESSER, MARCH 22, 1978: Dave Bierman observed a nocturnal light.

DRESSER, EARLY SEPTEMBER 1979: Five men said they saw a large, football-shaped object with a brilliant metallic sheen. One of the witnesses, an anonymous 25-year-old Army veteran who worked at a ski resort, was driving north at about 10:45 a.m. on County MM in Osceola Township, two miles east of Dresser in Polk County, when he saw a small, dark object above the tree line about a half-mile away. The object closed to within 200 meters of the car. The witness pulled over and left the car, and was joined by a passing trucker. The two men watched the object climb 200 feet and move over nearby East Lake. The trucker said that he and three others later saw the object again, near a gravel pit where he worked. It ascended into a clear sky at about an 85-degree angle.

DURAND, SEPT. 7, 1966: Mrs. E. Bruns had a close encounter of the first kind 10 miles east of town.

DURAND, JAN. 21, 1975: Scott Fedie had a close encounter of the first kind four miles southwest of town. The next evening Mitchell Doverspike observed a nocturnal light five miles to the southeast. On Jan. 29 and Jan. 31, Mrs. Al Gund observed a nocturnal light.

EAGLE, JULY 7, 1947: R.J. Southey observed a daylight disc southeast of town.

EAGLE RIVER, MAY 28, 1976: Nocturnal light observed.

EAU CLAIRE, SEPT. 7, 1966: Earlier in this evening, police in nearby Durand had observed an object with flashing red, blue and white lights, headed towards Eau Claire. They notified the Eau Claire Police Department, and at 9:25 p.m. Eau Claire officers Carl Skamfer and Donald Brunn saw two such UFOs. Skamfer saw it first as he drove on Skyline Drive. He observed the object for 45 minutes. Later Brunn and a reporter saw a similar object to the northeast. The UFO seemed to be in a playful mood: It bobbled, hovered, darted, went away and came back several times.

EAU CLAIRE, NOV. 5, 1971: T. Frank observed a nocturnal light.

EAU CLAIRE, NOV. 13, 1975: Nocturnal light observed.

EDGERTON, JULY 4, 1947, 11 P.M.: Mrs. Melvin Voight observed a nocturnal light, which she described as "an orange ball of light ... as big around as a barrel." Mrs. Voight was sitting in her car, which had broken down, while her husband went for help. "It scared the devil out of me when I saw it," she said. "I was all alone and didn't know what was happening when I saw something that looked at first like an opening in the sky. The disc had a sort of orange color. It was a round shape and it moved fast across the sky. It moved back again for about 10 minutes and then it disappeared all of a sudden. ... There was no light coming from Earth that could have done that." This was one of the first UFO sightings in the state.

ELKHORN, JULY 7, 1947: Kenneth Jones observed a daylight disc 10 miles from the city.

ELLSWORTH, DEC. 11, 1957: A close encounter of the first kind.

ELLSWORTH, MAY 13, 1976, 9 P.M.: Mr. and Mrs. Walter Beiga had a close encounter of the first kind. They had another four days later, at 9:15 p.m. On May 30, at 10:30 p.m., they had yet another, and managed to photograph the UFO.

ELLSWORTH, OCT. 21, 1980, 8:30 P.M.: A nocturnal light was observed by the Rev. and Mrs. Edward Groop and their son, by Alan and Marty Dikkers, and by Pat Kielas.

ELMWOOD, MARCH 2, 1975: While driving at about 8 p.m. the

Alfred "Bud" Forster family saw a particularly bright star. It seemed to be following them, but then stars and planets do seem to hold position relative to moving vehicles because of the objects' great distance. After a while the family decided the object was a satellite, as it seemed to be moving lower in the sky. Then the object settled in front of the car. It seemed to be landing. The object now appeared to be about the size of a car. It resembled two saucers put together, white, with lights all around. Underneath were sticklike legs. The children were screaming with fright, so the family fled, honking the car horn. As they did, the object left. This alerted Roger Weber, who lived on a nearby farm, and the Weber family observed the object as it flew away. Roger Weber guided the Forster family home, driving ahead of them. The whole time, the object was visible in the distance.

EMERY TOWNSHIP (PRICE COUNTY), DEC. 5, 1978, 3:40 P.M.: Rossann Boehm saw and photographed a daylight disc. It was seen at the same time, from another location, by Owen Hainy.

EVANSVILLE, NOV. 27, 1950: A commercial pilot and flight instructor, Bill Blair, watched six elliptical UFOs flying in loose echelon formation. The objects made a sound similar to that of helicopters, and appeared to be traveling about 500 m.p.h. at an altitude of 10,000 feet.

FARMERSVILLE (DODGE COUNTY), SOMETIME IN DECEMBER 1977, 8 P.M.: An anonymous freelance photographer took a picture of an unusual, unidentified flying object—something that by definition is a UFO. But the photographer told the *Fond du Lac Reporter* that he doubted that "the object in the photo was a flying saucer."

FENNIMORE, NOV. 5, 1975: Nocturnal light observed.

FENNIMORE, SEPT. 20, 1979, 5:30 A.M.: Guerdon Gratz had a close encounter of the second kind; the UFO gave off an odor of sulphur.

FLINTVILLE (BROWN COUNTY), APRIL 10, 1975: Nocturnal light observed.

FOND DU LAC, SEPT. 10, 1978: Harland Olsen and his wife had a close encounter of the first kind on Timber Trails Road.

FOOTVILLE, APRIL 16, 1978: A daylight disc was observed on County B.

FOREST COUNTY, SEPT. 10, 1980, 9:30 P.M.: In the area of Armstrong Creek, 23 miles east-northeast of Crandon, a nocturnal light at tree-top level was observed by witnesses from various locations, including Irene Eder and Gary Honeybuss.

FORT ATKINSON, LATE MARCH 1966: Police Capt. William Kapke and Officer Eugene Zechel, along with 15 other residents, saw an object as high as a star that was changing from green to white to red. "I don't care if anyone believes me or not," Zechel said. "I know it wasn't a star."

FORT ATKINSON, AUG. 25, 1972: Steve Cleveland experienced a close encounter of the third kind.

FORT ATKINSON, NOV. 13, 1975: Nocturnal light observed.

FREDERIC, DECEMBER 1974: Gunnard Linder observed a nocturnal light. (On Dec. 2 William Bosak reported his combined UFO-Bigfoot sighting; see Bigfoot chapter.)

FREDERIC, FEB. 24, 1975: Ray Kurkowski observed a nocturnal light at the Slush Pump Bar. (No jokes, please.)

GERMANTOWN, 1969: An eighth-grade boy and his brother saw a silver, luminous UFO over the treetops to the east of the dump. It was about a half mile away and appeared to be 75 feet in diameter. They watched it for about 15 seconds, when it was joined by a larger craft, estimated to be 150 to 200 feet in diameter. The larger UFO positioned itself over the smaller one. After another 15 seconds, the two UFOs vanished. The boys ran 60 to 70 feet toward their house, stopped and looked back to see that the UFOs had reappeared. The craft were now manuevering, making a series of right-angle turns. After 20 seconds, the UFOs again disappeared, this time for good.

GERMANTOWN, JULY 22, 1976: Nocturnal light observed.

GILLETT TOWNSHIP, MARCH 3, 1978: Edward Erickson observed a nocturnal light.

GILLS ROCK, SEPT. 13, 1959, 1:05 A.M.: Roland H. Daubner, 28, a paper maker, was outside looking for worms. He later told the Air Force, "I was outside only about five minutes when suddenly there was such a loud noise that it made my ears hurt. It sounded like a jet, only 10 times louder and pulsating. It seemed to stay right there in the field for a few seconds, and then [the sound] started to rise up. At this point I looked up and I saw the object. It looked like the bottom side of a [rocket], going straight up. It was a large yellowish, round ring of light with eight very bright blue lights just inside. ... Just inside the ring of blue lights was a ring of five red lights, much larger than the blue lights. The red lights seemed to flare up like a very hot exhaust. The object went straight up until it was out of sight." The combined sound/visual event lasted about 10 minutes. Daubner estimated that the object was two miles away. The sky was clear, there was no moon, the air was warm and dry, and there was no wind. After its investigation, the Air Force listed the object as unknown.

GORDON (DOUGLAS COUNTY), SEPT. 4, 1978, 12:15 A.M.: A 43-year-old university professor and his daughter had a close encounter of the first kind.

GRAFTON, NOV. 22, 1961, 7 P.M.: Honeywell metallurgist Melvin Vagle and his wife and son were traveling on Highway 81, approaching Grafton, when they saw a red light in the sky to the west. Other lights gradually joined it. The Vagles pulled over and watched. The largest object proved to be "a cigar-shaped object hovering at a sharp angle over a plowed field." Each tip of the cigar-shaped craft had a bright white light. The light on the upper end was steady; on the lower, blinking. Along the object's fuselage was a row of square ports, from which issued yellow light. The Vagles left when their son started crying. Earlier that evening a Grafton farmer had observed a similar object for 10 minutes.

GRAFTON, AUG. 5, 1979, 7 P.M.: A 38-year-old Chicago man observed nocturnal lights.

GREEN BAY, JULY 2, 1947, 6:30 P.M.: Eugene LaPlant and his son, Duane, observed a daylight disc. They were working in their garden when they noticed the rapidly moving silver ball. They watched it for three to four minutes as it moved to the northwest. Plant said it "definitely was not an airplane."

GREEN BAY, OCT. 5, 1958: Milford Vickman sighted a pulsating fireball.

GREEN BAY, AUG. 1-3, 1965: Mrs. Jack Lackman observed nocturnal lights.

GREEN BAY, NOV. 4, 1967: Nocturnal light observed.

GREEN BAY, DEC. 21, 1967: Ed Batz experienced a close encounter of the first kind.

GREEN BAY, JULY 23, 1978: At 4:25 a.m. Greenwich time, Green Bay Lighthouse, in response to a call made to Lake Michigan Coast Guard Stations originating at Coast Guard Station Ludington, Mich., reported seeing a UFO headed west. It had red and white lights and moved at a high rate of speed. The white light was very bright and flashed irregularly. Observation was handed off to Coast

Guard Station Two Rivers, Minn., at 4:45. This report was received from the Coast Guard through a Freedom of Information Act request. Coast Guard Station Sturgeon Bay made a similar observation at the same time.

GREENBUSH, JUNE 25, 1976, BEGINNING AT 1:20 A.M.: Many witnesses in different places observed a nocturnal light.

GREENFIELD, AUG. 9, 1975: Close encounter of the first kind.

GREENFIELD, SOMETIME IN 1977 OR 1978, AROUND 9:30 P.M.: A husband and wife were driving west on Layton Avenue. Near South 95th Street they saw a UFO that looked very much like the "Venusian Scout Craft" so often photographed by George Adamski, first of the celebrated (and discredited) 1950s contactees (see "Abducted!" chapter).

GREEN LAKE, APRIL 27, 1967: Nocturnal light observed.

GRESHAM, JUNE 22-25, 1972: Colin Lawe observed a nocturnal light on Highway 45. The object, or one like it, was seen on Highway 29 on July 29, and on County U on Nov. 24.

GRESHAM, AUG. 30, 1972: Close encounter of the second kind.

HAYWARD, AUG. 14, 1975: Nocturnal light observed.

HAZEL GREEN, APRIL 11, 1960, 5:50 P.M.: Mary Jo Curwen and others saw three saucer-shaped objects flying in a zig-zag fashion. Curwen had been filming family scenes in the barnyard, and she had the presence of mind to turn the camera onto the UFOs. Her 8mm color film was given to the Air Force almost immediately. The Air Force returned a copy of the film. This was then forwarded to the National Investigations Committee on Aerial Phenomena (NICAP), which analyzed it in Minneapolis and New York labs. NICAP's report: "The film was worthless as evidence of UFOs. The images were tiny, almost merging with the grain of the film, showed no appreciable motion other than typical movie film 'jump,' and were also visible in other scenes against the ground." NICAP held out the possibility that the report itself was true, but that the attempt to film the objects failed and that the family subsequently mistook film scratches for the objects.

HORTONVILLE, SEPT. 26, 1972: Nocturnal light observed.

HUBERTUS (WASHINGTON COUNTY), NOV. 4, 1977, 2:30 P.M.: Pat Mohan had a close encounter of the second kind. She and her family looked for traces, such as landing marks, that same day, and could not find any. But coincidentally—or perhaps not—she reported that there was an area in a field an eighth of a mile away from her house where nothing would grow, even as late as 1981. Investigator Don Schmidt said that the lack of growth was caused by "nitrogen burn."

HUDSON, AUG. 25, 1979, 10:30 P.M.: Four people experienced a close encounter of the first kind.

HULL (PORTAGE COUNTY), DEC. 12, 1980, 9 P.M.: Geraldine R. Shields, 15, and another girl sighted a nocturnal light.

HURLEY, OCT. 15, 1961: Daylight disc observed.

HUSTISFORD, FEB. 1, 1993, 8:15 P.M.: A Dodge County farmer reported a strange light to the Dodge County Sheriff's Department. The responding deputies saw an intense light that faded in and out as it moved westward. It was about 45 degrees above the horizon. They followed it for 20 miles, along Wisconsin 60. Near County BB, about two and a half miles east of Columbus, the object took a sudden turn left. The deputies were never able to get beneath it. As they approached the Jefferson County line they notified their colleagues there and ended the pursuit. Jefferson County deputies, however, did not report seeing it. The farmer who made the initial report said the object had a dome, which issued a bright light. Darker yellow lights beamed from the ends of the cigar-shaped hull. Madison and Milwaukee radar reported that there was no air traffic of any kind in the area at the time. Seven days earlier a similar sighting had been made by farmer Ray Stubinsky and his 14-year-old grandson, less than a mile outside Dodge County, in neighboring Waukesha County.

IRON RIDGE, JAN. 8, 1959: Mrs. Earl Becker sighted a daylight disc.

JANESVILLE, JULY 5, 1947: Mr. and Mrs. Al Sievert and Mr. and Mrs. Howard Roth spotted a nocturnal light. It seemed to be flying in ovals. It finally flew northwest at a "terrific speed," growing tails as it disappeared from view.

JANESVILLE, FEB. 13, 1969: Bill Leitz saw a nocturnal light five miles south of the city.

JOHNSBURG (FOND DU LAC COUNTY), AUG. 7, 1976, 10 P.M.: Orville Ziegelbauer and his son, Mark, had a close encounter of the third kind. An hour later the same UFO, or one like it, was seen south of Dotyville, about 13 miles from the initial sighting.

JORDAN CENTER (GREEN COUNTY), NOV. 30, 1978, FROM 5:15 TO 7:15 A.M.: Christine Figi and her daughter observed a UFO.

KENOSHA, JAN. 24, 1973: Francis J. Reich observed a nocturnal light over Lake Michigan, near Highway 32.

KENOSHA, JULY 6, 1978: Nocturnal light observed.

KRONENWETTER TOWNSHIP (MARATHON COUNTY), DEC. 26, 1978, 6:15 P.M.: A group observed a nocturnal light.

LA CROSSE, APRIL 14, 1952, 12:35 P.M.: An airline pilot observed several light-colored objects flying in "V" formation. The sighting was investigated by the Air Force, which listed it as unknown.

LA CROSSE, JUNE 5, 1976: Close encounter of the first kind.

LA CROSSE, OCT. 9, 1982: Three people observed a nocturnal light.

LA CROSSE, MARCH 3-4, 1993: Four adults and four children in West Salem, on the south side of La Crosse, saw a bright light displaying a crosslike pattern, with moving multicolored lights. The shape of the object was not clear, and witnesses estimated that it was about a mile away. The next day, a husband and wife saw an oblong saucer at 8 p.m., hovering over the Mormon Coulee Cemetery. It was shining a bright light on the ground. It moved north, then south, then displayed a red, oscillating light.

LA CROSSE, AUG. 21, 1995, 2 A.M.: A trucker witnessed a "big orange ball" flying directly toward him from the south. The object suddenly "split into five pieces" and disappeared.

LADYSMITH, JUNE 14, 1957: A.W. Daniels observed a nocturnal light.

LADYSMITH, JAN. 23, 1995, 11:42 P.M.: Personnel at the Rusk County Sheriff's Department observed a hovering light in the southeast sky.

LA FARGE, SEPT. 6, 1979, 10:30 P.M.: John and Barbara Madden and their son observed a nocturnal light.

LAKE "KISHKANOUG," JUNE 28, 1952, 6 P.M.: G. Metcalfe observed a silver sphere, which turned and became an ellipse, suggesting a platter shape. The object then flew up and away, very quickly. The sighting lasted about 10 seconds, and was investigated by the Air Force, which lists it as unexplained. (Air Force files list the locale as Lake "Kishkanoug," but I can find no reference to such a lake in Wisconsin; I believe it actually is Lake Koshkonong in Jefferson County.)

LAKE KOSHKONONG, SPRING 1971: UFO observed.

LAKE MICHIGAN, EARLY AUGUST 1952: A TWA captain told Donald Keyhoe, head of the civilian UFO investigative agency

NICAP, that he had been flying his airliner over the lake when "a lighted disc buzzed it." The pilot refused to report the sighting to the Air Force, for fear of ridicule.

LAKE SUPERIOR, NOV. 7, 1951: A steamship captain and crew observed an elongated orange object with six rows of two glowing "portholes" on each side. It was flying east.

LAKE SUPERIOR, AUG. 13, 1952: An Air Force radar base on the Keweenaw Peninsula of Michigan watched a flight of UFOs over the lake.

LAKE SUPERIOR, AUGUST 1975: The same Air Force radar base tracked 10 UFOs on radar over the lake, moving from southwest to northeast at 9,000 miles an hour. Seven other UFOs then appeared over Duluth, Minn. Jet interceptors were sent to intercept them, but were outdistanced.

LAKE WINNEBAGO, OCT. 27, 1979, 10:30 P.M.: Several people saw a nocturnal light streak over the lake, then explode. (I believe this was probably a meteor.)

LANCASTER, NOV. 4, 1975: Close encounter of the first kind.

LOMIRA, OCT. 18, 1974: Bob Kuehn and another person had a close encounter of the first kind.

LONE ROCK, SEPT. 28, 1976: Daylight disc sighted.

LUCK, APRIL 14, 1996: A husband and wife saw a cluster of bright lights pass from southwest to northeast, beneath clouds. The cluster left a "beautiful tail of light." Similar sightings were made in the area; in nearby St. Cloud, Minn., the object seen was described as a large "trapezoid of very bright amber lights with strobes."

MADISON: See "Take Me to Your Leader" chapter for Madison sightings.

MARINETTE COUNTY, AUG. 30 OR 31, 1980, 9 P.M.: In the southern part of the county, near the Peshtigo River, a "red ball with a cone-shaped red light going about it" was observed by two people. The UFO appeared over the tree line to the northwest, and through binoculars appeared to be the size of a basketball. It rose straight up and then slowly dropped. It shrank considerably in size and then sped to the west.

MARION, JAN. 13, 1973: A nocturnal light was observed near County G and Highway 110.

MARSHFIELD, APRIL 28, 1976: Nocturnal light observed.

MASON, FEB. 11, 1981: Nocturnal light observed.

MATTOON, MARCH 2, 1975: Jim Zahn observed a nocturnal light.

MAUSTON JULY 5, 1979, 2:30 OR 3 P.M.: Beaulah Johnson saw a UFO.

MELLEN, MARCH 13-14, 1975: The Baker family had a close encounter of the second kind (see "The 1975 UFO Wave" chapter).

MENASHA, JUNE 26, 1978, JUST BEFORE 11 P.M.: Frank and Virginia Adrian saw a nocturnal light on Broad Street. At the same time, John Q. Mitchell observed two nocturnal lights.

MENASHA, AUG. 13, 1978, JUST AFTER 10 P.M.: Judie Fingal observed a nocturnal light and photographed it. In the picture, the small light that was seen appeared as a bright streak.

MENASHA, 1975 TO 1986: Bonnie Meyer and Judie Woolcott claimed in 1986 that they had been abducted by aliens at least seven times in 11 years. They said that their memories of the events had been blocked, but that hypnosis had recalled them. Meyer said that during at least one abduction she was taken from her family while sleeping. She tried to call for help, but the family had been placed in "suspended animation" by the aliens. During one of the encounters, the two women said, they traveled 93 minutes to another planet.

MENOMINEE COUNTY, JULY 30, 1972: Nocturnal light observed.

MENOMONEE FALLS, NOV. 14, 1964, 9:40 P.M.: Dr. R.G. Wagner and two girls saw three dim reddish lights fly through a 160-degree arc in five to six seconds. The sighting was investigated by the Air Force, which listed it as unknown.

MENOMONEE FALLS, JULY 6, 1977, FROM 9 TO 11 P.M.: Linda, Lynore and Pennie Wiler observed nocturnal lights.

MENOMONEE FALLS, MARCH 10, 1981, 7:55 P.M.: A nocturnal light with a long tail was observed by two witnesses in different locations. It appeared to be flying level to the west at a height of 2,000 to 3,000 feet, much faster than any jet. The object was in sight for eight seconds.

MEQUON, THE NIGHT OF DEC. 31, 1980: Two people driving south saw a light near Cedarburg Road that looked a great deal like a streetlight, except there were no streetlights there.

MIDDLETON, SEPT. 28, 1978: Joel Ward saw a nocturnal light in the 8000 block of Mineral Point Road (also see chapter on Madison UFOs).

MILTON, JULY 7, 1947: Paul Schroeder observed a daylight disc.

MILWAUKEE, JUNE 28, 1947: That evening a woman reported to the Air Force that she had seen 10 flying saucers flying "like blue blazes" over her house. They were headed south. This and the following reports are among the first in the state.

MILWAUKEE, JULY 5, 1947: Nocturnal lights were seen by Frank Phifer, a guest at the Pfister Hotel. He said he saw three balls of fire shooting across Lake Michigan, "going at terrific speed." They were also seen by Mr. and Mrs. Anthony Hoffman on the 3000 block of West Layton Avenue (she described the lights as looking like "a small meat platter"); by William Humphrey on the 3000 block of South 20th Street; and by Glen Bowden, again at Mitchell Field.

MILWAUKEE, JULY 6, 1947: Passengers of an airliner arriving at night at Mitchell Field saw a flying saucer bobbing over the airport as they left the plane. John Bosch had earlier sighted two daylight discs over the airport. At 6 p.m. Erwin Rottman saw three, with tails. The UFOs turned from orange to gold and then to silver. Another was sighted on July 8 by an anonymous witness.

MILWAUKEE, APRIL 26, 1952: Five discs were observed over the city.

MILWAUKEE, APRIL 29, 1952: UFO observed.

MILWAUKEE, JAN. 16, 1962: Mrs. Norbert J. Schoeneman saw a nocturnal light near South 43rd Street and West Oklahoma Avenue.

MILWAUKEE, AROUND 1965: A man saw flashing lights in the fog ahead of his car. The engine failed, and the lights flew up into the air and vanished.

MILWAUKEE, AROUND 1970: Berna Richter and two others experienced a close encounter of the first kind.

MILWAUKEE, FALL 1974 OR 1975: On the city's south side, nine-year-old Richard H. was walking home from school with another boy when a UFO appeared, 30 to 40 feet overhead. Richard said he felt like it was "drawing him up out of his head." He chose not to talk about it to a UFO investigator. The sighting was reported by Richard's mother, who apologized for her son's lack of cooperation. Also in 1974 or 1975, nine-year-old Karen G. was walking in Concordia Park, on Milwaukee's west side, when she had a close encounter of the first kind. It was reported by her mother.

MILWAUKEE, 1975: George Koleas had a close encounter of the first kind.

MILWAUKEE, JAN. 29, 1975: Nocturnal light observed.

MILWAUKEE, JULY 10, 1975: Nocturnal light observed.

MILWAUKEE, AUG. 17, 1975: Nocturnal light observed.

MILWAUKEE, SEPT. 7, 1979, JUST BEFORE 8:30 P.M.: Bruce Szewczuga and Randall Froschheuser observed a nocturnal light over the city's southwest side.

MILWAUKEE, OCT. 10, 1995, 7:45 P.M.: A man on Highway 43, southwest of Milwaukee, saw a large bright-blue light streak by his car, descend, turn and cross the road ahead of him. It seemed to strobe.

MINOCQUA, NOV. 25, 1980, 10:30 P.M.: At nearby Lake Tomahawk two nocturnal lights were observed by Ruth Klippel, Dale Kroh, Celeste Nowak and a police officer.

MONONA, SEPT. 8, 1970: Mrs. Richard Hodges observed a nocturnal light two miles to the east. (See "Take Me to Your Leader" chapter.)

MONROE, FEB. 3, 1953: Nocturnal light observed.

MONROE, APRIL 11, 1978: Nocturnal light observed two miles northwest on Highway 81.

MONROE, FEB. 25, 1979, FROM 7 TO 7:30 P.M.: Numerous witnesses in the area saw nocturnal lights, which also appeared on radar.

MONTELLO, MAY 18, 1972: Nocturnal light observed.

MONTICELLO, APRIL 3, 1964, 9 P.M.: R. Wold, a graduate student in anthropology, was driving west on County C, towards Argyle, with his wife, mother-in-law and 12-year-old sister-in-law. It was quite dark—they did not see any stars or the quarter moon. But one mile out of town they did see two red blinking lights at about 11 o'clock. They speculated that the lights were coming from a police car on a distant hill. The witnesses drove closer, though, and realized that the lights were too high to be coming from a police car and that their car was going to pass beneath them. They then believed the lights were coming from an airliner, which was about to crash. The witnesses stopped, rolled down the car windows, and turned off the headlights. The mother said they should get out. The girl fell to the floor in the back seat and tried to hide. The object came closer, slowing, finally hovering alongside their car, but about 100 yards to their left. The two lights had become four, posted like corners on a rectangle, with one white light "in front of the others"—in three dimensions, its shape was like a squat nail with a broad, square head. There were also many other lesser lights, which they only were able to observe at the object's closest approach. The witnesses saw the object pass behind telephone poles and wires—it was at about a 30-degree elevation now, coming so close that the driver thought it could just barely fit between the poles. They never did make out a solid hull or other structure; only the fact that the lights moved and retained their relationship to each other made the witnesses believe that the lights were fastened to a larger whole. They did have an impression, however, that the red lights were reflecting dimly off a polished surface. The UFO passed just to the rear of the car. The husband started the car and turned on the lights. He drove ahead, into a farm driveway, as the object began to leave. It was moving quickly and he wanted to chase it. They did, at up to 50 mph, but they lost it as it moved in the direction of Monticello. The whole experience had lasted between five and 10 minutes. The sighting was investigated by the Air Force, which listed it as unknown.

MORRISONVILLE (DANE COUNTY), JULY 1, 1947, 7:30 P.M.: An anonymous housewife told the *Capital Times* in Madison that she and her husband had seen an oblong flying saucer. "I was puzzled," she said. "My husband, an overseas veteran, insisted it was an aluminum airplane! I couldn't imagine what else it could be, and couldn't help but wonder why there wasn't a motor running. ... I know what doctors and scientists say about people who say they have seen them. But how can this be an hallucination?"

MOSINEE, MAY 29, 1968: Close encounter of the second kind.

MUKWONAGO, OCT. 14, 1973: A couple, "Nancy and Jim," had a close encounter of the third kind at nearby Phantom Lakes.

NEILLSVILLE, APRIL 23, 1976: Nocturnal light observed.

NEILLSVILLE, OCT. 19, 1977, ABOUT 8 P.M.: An object with "white, green and yellow lights, ports that looked like windows, and a red light on a pointed tail" was sighted by 11 people. It appeared at treetop level.

NEW BERLIN, JULY 28, 1975: Nocturnal light observed.

NEW GLARUS, SEPT. 1, 1979, 3:30 A.M.: Three sheriff's deputies observed nocturnal lights.

NEW RICHMOND, SEPT. 4, 1979, 7:30 P.M.: An elderly couple observed a nocturnal light southwest of town. At 7:45 p.m., it was spotted at a much closer distance by three men, a sighting that placed the UFO into the daylight disc category.

NORTH HUDSON, MARCH 1, 1976: Nocturnal light observed.

NORTH PRAIRIE, JUNE 17, 1979, 10 P.M.: A businessman observed a nocturnal light.

OKAUCHEE (WAUKESHA COUNTY), JULY 7, 1947: Daylight disc observed by Charles Pettit.

OMRO, OCT. 15, 1973: George Willis had a so-called close encounter of the fourth kind—abduction.

OMRO, AUG. 10, 1989, 3:30 A.M.: Karen Sazama and Gary Michael Frye, while fishing on the Fox River and Lake Butte des Morts, saw "an orange-reddish light." The light stayed in the sky for 20 to 25 minutes. "I really got scared out there," Sazama told the Associated Press. "I was looking for a place to hide in the boat." She described it as bigger than a star, moving with a falling motion. The two caught no fish—they thought the light may have had something to do with that—and they reported the incident to the Winnebago Sheriff's Department five hours later.

OCONOMOWOC TOWNSHIP, JAN. 26, 8 P.M.: Farmer Ray Stubinsky and his 14-year-old grandson saw lights very near the ground. The lights were in a cornfield, "too low to be a tractor," Ray Stubinsky said. The lights approached and the farmer saw three "machines" arranged vertically, in pyramid fashion. Stubinsky was sure they weren't helicopters, and after being told of a UFO sighted a week later in Hustisford, said that they didn't resemble the latter object, either.

OCONOMOWOC, SEPT. 16, 1979, EARLY MORNING: Reporters at the *Waukesha Freeman* heard something interesting come over their police scanner—chatter about two men who were "hurt by a spacecraft," photos of which were taken. I could not get any confirmation of the report.

ORFORDVILLE, MAY 4, 1976: Close encounter of the first kind.

OSCEOLA, JULY 29, 1952, 1:30 A.M.: Radar operators on the ground and the pilot of an airborne propellor-driven P-51 Mustang together made this rare "radar/visual" sighting, a type of report that to many UFO researchers presents irrefutable evidence. In this case, several clusters of as many as 10 small targets and one large one were "painted" by ground radar. The smaller targets moved from southwest to east at 60 to 70 mph, one following the other. After a jet interceptor was sent up to investigate, the larger target moved considerably faster, at 700 mph. The other pilot, in the P-51, observed one of the objects. The event's duration was one hour. This report was investigated by the Air Force, which listed it as unexplained.

OSCEOLA, MARCH 22, 1978: Neil Johnson saw a nocturnal light four miles south of town.

OSCEOLA, DEC. 4, 1980, 6 P.M.: Rodney Wycoff and Terry Enney observed nocturnal lights.

OSCEOLA, SUMMER 1983: Bill Benson saw an object "the size of four blimps" over three-mile Long Lake. The object was darker than the sky and rimmed with orange lights. It hovered silently for several minutes. "I don't know what it is, but whatever it was, it was big," he told the Associated Press. In the same area, in August 1988, dairy farmer John Dins had seen a 100-foot object over his silo at 11:15 p.m. He had just finished milking his cows and was herding them outside when they "bolted" back into the barn. "What the heck happened to them?" he thought. Dins exited, saw the object and ran to wake his wife and three daughters. "I thought, 'Geez, I've got to get somebody out to see this.' " When they got outside, the object had moved to the eastern horizon. That same night Duane Schmid was working at Regal Ware Inc. in Kewaskum. He and co-workers were eating outside when six orange lights appeared above them. The lights went out one by one. Schmid said it was his 15th UFO sighting. "You can't explain it away. It was there," he said.

OSHKOSH, JAN. 27, 1964: UFO seen over Lake Winnebago.

OTTAWA (WAUKESHA COUNTY), THE NIGHT OF SEPT. 20, 1978: A UFO that looked something like a boat was observed.

PALMYRA, AROUND 1943: Daylight disc observed.

PARK FALLS, JULY 17, 1977, 3 A.M.: Mr. and Mrs. Ken JuVette and their daughter observed a nocturnal light.

PARK FALLS, MAY 25, 1978, 10:15 P.M.: Stephen M. Vuchetich had a close encounter of the first kind near Butternut Lake.

PATCH GROVE, NOV. 6, 1975: Harold Posten observed a nocturnal light.

PEPIN, NOVEMBER 1945: Close encounter of the third kind.

PHILLIPS, MARCH 2, 1975: Close encounter of the first kind.

PICKETT (WINNEBAGO COUNTY), JAN. 3, 1981, 6:45 P.M.: A woman observed a nocturnal light.

PLAIN, JULY 14, 1975: Nocturnal light observed.

PLATTEVILLE, JAN. 28, 1977: Nocturnal light observed.

PLOVER, AUG. 21, 1972: Jack West observed a nocturnal disc on

Highway 51 and the Beltline in Madison (see "Take Me to Your Leader" chapter).

PLYMOUTH, SPRING 1976: Two men and three boys in a car had a close encounter of the first kind on Highway 57.

PRAIRIE DU CHIEN, OCT. 19, 1967: Michael Leyh was watching TV when two women came to his door and urged him to come out. Once outside, all three saw a domed, oval-shaped craft, about the size of a car and spurting flame, about 40 feet overhead. It moved north and disappeared a few miles outside the city. At least 19 people in all saw the UFO.

PRAIRIE DU CHIEN, SEPT. 6, 1978, FROM 8:45 TO 10:15 P.M.: Dozens of witnesses in the city, and across the Mississippi River in McGregor, Iowa, observed nocturnal lights.

PRICE COUNTY, NOV. 3, 1960: Some small boys said they encountered a small, warm UFO.

PRINCETON, MARCH 1, 1996: A man saw a large circular orange light. A few minutes later he saw a "bizarre" cluster of lights, blinking sequentially.

RACINE, JULY 7, 1947: Nocturnal light observed.

RACINE, APRIL 7, 1952, 4:40 A.M.: Nocturnal light observed. It was fiery, green and spherical, and was trailed by short streamers of red and yellow. It crossed the sky and disappeared over the horizon.

RACINE, NOV. 27, 1965: Nocturnal light observed.

RACINE, MARCH 14, 1982: Two people experienced a close encounter of the first kind.

RACINE, JULY 28, 1995, 2 P.M.: A husband and wife saw a very bright silver disc in the clear sky. It was suddenly joined by two identical craft.

RED CLIFF, THE NIGHT OF DEC. 30, 1979: A falling object was reported, believed by some to be a plane and by others to be a meteor.

RHINELANDER, FEBRUARY 1978: Nocturnal light observed by Shirley Peters.

RHINELANDER, LATE 1981: Chrystal Jackson, an artist who has contributed to *National Geographic* magazine, was asleep in the back of a car that was traveling north near the city, when her son, Chris, saw a starlike object over a field. "He woke me up and I was amazed," she said. "And then it followed us for about 10 minutes. I hope people don't make too much fun of me about this. I feel very serious about it."

RICE LAKE, AROUND JANUARY 1979: Craig and Carolyn Greener observed a daylight disc.

RICE LAKE, SEPT. 10, 1980, 9 P.M.: Mark and Michelle Gonske and a group of children observed nocturnal lights.

RICHLAND CENTER, LATE MARCH 1966: Lt. Fred Bayer of the Sauk County Sheriff's Department said he saw a high-flying UFO twice. It had no discernible shape and varied in color. A similar sighting was reported in Mauston.

RIPON, APRIL 19, 1965: A nocturnal light was observed over a drive-in theater.

ST. CROIX FALLS, OCT. 10, 1951: J.J. Kaliszewski saw a daylight disc 10 miles east of the city.

ST. CROIX FALLS, APRIL 12, 1952: UFO observed.

ST. CROIX FALLS, JULY 1976: Nocturnal light observed on St. Croix Road.

ST. CROIX FALLS, MARCH 22, 1978: Lorena McClain saw a nocturnal light from State Road.

SHAWANO, JULY 29, 1972: A UFO was spotted in Shawano, Waupaca, Outagamie and Brown counties. Members of sheriff's departments in the first two counties were among the witnesses. One officer described the object as appearing bright orange and about the size of a volleyball from a distance of two or three miles. It was moving at a height of 800 feet and followed a zig-zag pattern across the sky.

SHAWANO COUNTY, JULY 29, 1972: Nocturnal light observed.

SHEBOYGAN, NOV. 23, 1960: Nocturnal light observed.

SHEBOYGAN, MARCH 24, 1966: Close encounter of the first kind.

SOMERSET, MAY 2, 1978: Nocturnal light observed.

SPARTA, AUGUST 1972: Ray Harris saw a nocturnal light on County Q.

SPOONER, MARCH 29, 1953, 3:45 P.M.: R.H. Daubner observed a round yellow light with eight blue lights within it, and then five larger red lights, fly up very fast. The object or objects made a pulsating noise like that made by a jet engine. The sighting lasted 10 minutes. It was investigated by the Air Force, which listed it as unknown.

SPOONER, NOV. 4, 1957: Daylight disc observed.

SPOONER, AUGUST 1978: Apparent landing marks found.

STANLEY, JULY 18, 1962, 8 P.M.: Mrs. Florence Cummins saw something odd. She reached for her 7x35 binoculars and made out two objects shaped sort of like dumbbells—thick bars with bulging ends. Both UFOs were bright silver, clear and sharply outlined. The "rear" object glowed red underneath. The objects traveled from south to southwest at about 20 to 30 degrees elevation. There was no sound, trail or exhaust.

STEVENS POINT, JULY 8, 1947: Daylight disc observed.

STEVENS POINT, NOVEMBER 1971: Close encounter of the first kind.

STOUGHTON, JULY 7, 1947, AROUND SUNDOWN: Mr. and Mrs. Morris Nicholls and their son-in-law and daughter, Mr.and Mrs. Gerhard Schedel, saw a strange, shiny object in the sky east of Stoughton. "It appeared somewhat like an airplane, and it moved like an airplane but made no noise," said Mrs. Nicholls, whose first name was not recorded by the reporter from Madison's *Capital Times*. She believed that the object, whatever it was, passed over the Skaalen Home for the Aged, north of town. Late the next day, Mr. and Mrs. John Ovren and their daughter, Mrs. Lawrence Wene, reported seeing a golden flashing disc north of their cottage, which was situated on Lake Kegonsa. The object appeared to be hovering low near the center of the lake, appearing and disappearing in the sky. John Ovren tried unsuccessfully to identify the object through binoculars. He said he believed that it was an aircraft—despite its peculiar behavior.

STOUGHTON 1967: Richard Dvorak observed a nocturnal light on Highway 57.

STRUM, NOV. 11, 1957: Daylight disc observed.

STURGEON BAY, SUMMER 1947: Ronald Larsen observed a nocturnal light.

STURGEON BAY, MAY 21, 1952: Coral Lorenzen saw a daylight disc near Third Avenue.

STURGEON BAY, FEB. 21-23, 1953: Nocturnal lights observed.

STURGEON BAY, NOV. 4, 1967: UFO observed.

STURGEON BAY, SEPT. 6, 1970: Apparent landing marks found.

STURGEON BAY, AUG. 6, 1975: Nocturnal light observed.

SUN PRAIRIE, DEC. 1, 1970: Nocturnal light observed by Jan Peterson.

TIGERTON, JULY 29, 1972: Dennis Kussman saw a nocturnal light near Highway 45 and County M.

TOMAHAWK, JUNE 17, 1878, 11 P.M.: Nocturnal light observed.

TWIN LAKES, AUG. 14, 1975: Nocturnal light observed.

TWO RIVERS, THE NIGHT OF JULY 27, 1978: Gary Randall, Doug Wangen and at least three others saw a nocturnal light at 11:57 p.m., 12:04 a.m. and 12:45 a.m., near the Coast Guard station. Randall took 10 photos of the UFO, and sent them to "a government agency in Milwaukee for studying." At 12:25 p.m. a similar sighting was made at the Green Bay lighthouse. At 11:45 p.m., Aug. 9, Tom Gordon of the Coast Guard and four or five others had a close encounter of the first kind at the Coast Guard station. It was, Gordon said, a "structured object that manuevered."

TWO RIVERS, SEPTEMBER 1978: Possible landing traces—a gray 10-foot diameter ring was found on the grass on a farm.

VERMONT, JAN. 5, 1986: Several residents of Iowa County, including Sheriff Nick Basting, saw a strange light. Jean and Bob Ellarson of rural Barneveld were driving west on Zwetler Road in Vermont at about 9:45 p.m. when they saw a motionless light. They stopped their car, rolled down a window, and "all of a sudden, the thing started coming toward us—and I mean fast," Jean Ellarson said. "It was like a big, bright star. There were no blinking lights, no red and green, like you might see on a plane, and there was no noise. It moved very fast, then swung off toward Highway 14. Sheriff Basting thought it was an airplane with its landing lights on. "I wouldn't swear to it, but that's what I think it was." He spotted it from his patrol car, south of Mineral Point, after seeing some flashing lights. He heard no noise and described the object's path as a straight line.

VIROQUA, OCT. 29, 1975: Close encounter of the first kind.

WALDO, JULY 13, 1976: A family observed a nocturnal light.

WALDO, APRIL 10, 1977: Twelve people observed a nocturnal light.

WALWORTH, JAN. 8, 1959: Gordon Higgins saw a daylight disc from Highway 14.

WASHBURN, JULY 8, 1975: Daylight disc observed.

WASHBURN, NOV. 2, 1975: Nocturnal light observed.

WASHBURN, APRIL 22, 1977: Nocturnal light observed.

WASHBURN, FALL 1979: "An unusual red light—the sort made by flares but stretching across the entire skyline"—was reported a year after the fact by the *Washburn Times*. There were, obviously, many witnesses.

WASHINGTON, AUG. 20, 1978: Several people saw a nocturnal light.

WAUPUN, EARLY APRIL 1974: Nocturnal light observed.

WAUKESHA COUNTY, JULY 3, 1947, 5 P.M.: Three Madisonians driving to Milwaukee were among the first in the state to see a UFO. The flying saucer craze had only begun a month earlier and was still so new that Boyle had not even heard about it. The witnesses were Ted Boyle, a member of the Madison Common Council, his mother and Ruth Donhard. Boyle described the UFO as a bright, silvery object, high over the north horizon. "It was shinier than the dickens," he said. "It was oval-shaped. We watched it for two or three minutes and then it disappeared all of a sudden. ... It kept the oval shape and then it seemed to flatten out, into a circular shape like a platter; then it disappeared all of a sudden." After arriving in Milwaukee, Boyle learned about the flying saucer phenomena and reported the sighting.

WAUKESHA COUNTY, 1966: Patricia Blake had a close encounter of the second kind on County JF.

WAUKESHA COUNTY, AUG. 21, 1972: Greg V. Faltersack's car stalled as he observed a UFO.

WAUKESHA COUNTY, SEPT. 15, 1979, 4 A.M.: Police observed a nocturnal light north of Wales.

WAUKESHA, DEC. 1, 1995, 5:20 P.M.: A woman in a car witnessed a "shooting star" with multiple lights descend vertically, suddenly stop and then shoot off horizontally. A very similar object was seen at 10:55 p.m. in Owosso, Mich., and at 1:40 p.m. in Orland Park, Ill.

WAUNAKEE, JULY 14, 1987: Police officers Kevin Plendl and Scott McElroy responded at around 2 a.m. to a report from a woman on Division Street that she had been viewing strange lights in the sky for about an hour. By the time they arrived, the object had disappeared. They waited, and the object returned suddenly. It "popped into" the sky, they said. According to Plendl, "It went from not being there" to there. The object was shaped like a half to quarter moon and had red and blue lights. At times it brightened and shifted in the sky from north to south. After watching for 15 to 20 minutes, the officers moved down River Road, three miles away, to change their view. Plendl said he was looking at the object through binoculars when he "saw something come flying off it. It went at a tremendous speed." He watched the part that came off but after a while lost sight of it. At around 4 a.m., the object itself disappeared. It did not return the next night. Despite the officers' unusual description and the object's failure to return to the sky the following evening, a University of Wisconsin research astronomer said that the object must have been the star Betelgeuse.

WAUPACA, AUGUST 1972: Nocturnal light observed.

WAUSAU, AUG. 22, 1965: UFO observed.

WAUSAU, MARCH 3, 1975: Nocturnal light observed.

WAUSAU, APRIL 6, 1975, 2 A.M.: Rod. S. and Mike L., two teenagers from Milwaukee, had a close encounter of the third kind. Afterward, they noticed that a period of time had elapsed that they could not account for, suggesting a close encounter of the fourth kind.

WAUSAU, DEC. 28, 1978: Bernice Rainville saw a nocturnal light from the 1400 block of South 26th Street.

WAUSHARA COUNTY, JAN. 3, 1981: At 7:30 p.m. and again from 8 to 10 p.m., unusual lights were observed across the county by numerous witnesses, including two sheriff's deputies.

WAUTOMA, JAN. 6, 1979: Richard Singles had a close encounter of the first kind.

WAUTOMA, JAN. 3, 1981, 8:10 P.M.: At least five people observed a nocturnal light six miles east of the city. Only witness Jerome Withney gave investigators his full name. Other witnesses were Clarence and Betty B., Blanche Van A. and Donna R.

WAUWATOSA, NOV. 10, 1975: Peter Eilbes had a close encounter of the third kind. Coincidentally, on this same night the Edmund Fitzgerald was lost.

WEST ALLIS, JAN. 12, 1967: Art Hoerres observed a daylight disc.

WEST ALLIS, JULY 4, 1976: Roger W. observed a nocturnal light.

WEST BEND, JUNE 15, 1973: Daniel Infalt and his daughter, Colleen, had a close encounter of the third kind at Little Cedar Lake, four miles south-southwest of the city.

WHITEFISH BAY, JUNE 24, 1950: A nocturnal light was observed southeast of the city.

WHITEWATER, NOV. 13, 1975: Nocturnal light observed.

WILD ROSE, DEC. 30, 1980, IN THE EARLY EVENING: Gary Firnges observed a nocturnal light east-southeast of town. He saw it again at 6:15 p.m. on Jan. 3, 1981.

WINTER, MAY 2, 1976: Dagmar Noel and her friend, Lloyd Pringle, were driving to Milwaukee on County M when they saw three deer along the road. They slowed down. From the *Sawyer County Gazette*, to whom Dagmar Noel later wrote: "All at once in front of them on the road was a machine that looked like a car, and yet it didn't look like one. It was sort of faded white or bluish. Lloyd later told [Dagmar] that he saw it following them but thought it was an odd-looking car. She slowed down again and then the machine stopped in the road and a person ran out—very fast. He ran as fast as a road runner about 200 feet ahead." The slender man was about 5 feet 6 inches tall and wore a dark-colored jump suit. As fast as he ran out of the vehicle, he turned and ran back. At that time, the witnesses saw a larger "space ship about 200 feet past the smaller machine. This machine was dark red—the shape was like a bowl upside down. It covered from one side of the road to the next. ... There were some dark markings and there was a little vapor or haze around it." Both objects simply disappeared from view.

WINTER, THE NIGHT OF NOV. 2, 1979: Joe Paulock and several others observed a nocturnal light.

WISCONSIN-ILLNOIS BORDER, SEPT. 20, 1979, 6 A.M.: Several drivers observed a UFO south of Monroe.

WISCONSIN-MINNESOTA BORDER, JULY 28, 1952: Air Force jets chased a UFO tracked by ground radar. The UFO sped away from the interceptors. The object's speed ranged from 60 to 600 mph.

WISCONSIN-MINNESOTA BORDER, THE NIGHT OF NOV. 26, 1965: This was a night of power failures for residents on both sides of the border. Beginning shortly after 8 p.m., an object with blinking blue lights was seen in and around St. Paul, Minn. It sent out occasional flashes of bright blue light. The UFO was observed by many, including police officers in Totem Town, Minn., who reported to the Northern States Power Company that the power failures plaguing the utility's customers that night coincided with the object's appearance. The utility could not explain the outages.

WISCONSIN-MINNESOTA BORDER, MARCH 22, 1978, BE-TWEEN 8:45 AND 9:15 P.M.: Dozens of witnesses reported a nocturnal light traveling roughly on a path from Cumberland in Barron County, Wis., to St. Paul, Minn.

ABDUCTED!

In the 1950s, even saucer buffs laughed at people who said they'd met the aliens. The cases involving "contactees" were too strange, too unlikely. And they frankly embarrassed those who wanted the larger UFO phenomena to receive serious scientific attention.

Today we call the contactees "abductees," and their numbers have grown so great and their experiences so common that the U.S. Department of Health and Human Services has taken up their case.

According to a 1991 Roper poll, surprisingly high numbers of U.S. citizens have experienced unusual and/or paranormal phenomena suggesting that they may be abductees: 18 percent said they had awakened "paralyzed with a sense of a strange person or presence or something else" in their room one or more times; 13 percent said they experienced "a period of time of an hour or more, in which [they] were apparently lost, but could not remember why, or where"; 10 percent felt at some time a sensation of actually flying, though they didn't know where, why or how; 8 percent had seen unusual, unexplainable lights or balls of light in a room; 8 percent reported discovering "puzzling scars" on their bodies that neither they "nor anyone else" remembered how or where they were inflicted.

Overall, 2 percent of Americans answered "yes" to four of the five questions above (which, per standard polling strategy, were included in much larger polls dealing with a mixture of lifestyle and behavioral questions). The results indicated that 3.7 million Americans exhibited signs suggesting that they have experienced the so-called alien abduction phenomena.

A former Wisconsinite, Donna Shalala, made the decision for governmental investigation. (Before she became President Bill Clinton's Secretary of Health and Human Services, Shalala was chancellor of the University of Wisconsin-Madison.) Since 1974, DHHS has required that people taking part in research experiments must first sign an Informed Consent Form. Since the aliens are not providing abductees with the form before performing experiments on them, well ...

In August 1994, Shalala assigned the abductees' cases to Lana R. Skirboll, director of the Office of Science Policy and Program Planning. Among the questions Skirboll has put to abductees in assembling her investigation:

"Can you describe the investigator performing the procedures? Did s/he state their name? (If the researchers looked human, then so state. Try to look beyond the paradoxical answers usually given, to an event that caused you to think that maybe you were, in fact, dealing with humans.)"

Skirboll has since left DHHS; Andrea Baruichin, associate director of Science Policy and Program Planning, has now taken over the project and has informed abductees that she will review the evidence so far. What is she likely to discover?

She'll probably find that abduction reports have practically become a fad, interwoven with various New Age philosophies. The stories center on the "grays," slight nude figures with slender limbs, teardrop heads and wrap-around eyes. The grays are evil, some say.

Several researchers refuse to classify the tales as "abductions," and instead set the stories next to reports of mysteriously slaughtered cattle and call them "human mutilations." That's because the abductees almost uniformly report that they are experimented on, operated on. The aliens—if they are aliens and not oddly evolved humans from the future, or characters from a parallel reality, or angels (more on that in a bit)—seem terribly interested in our reproduction process. They implant women, force sex between men and women, men and aliens, and women and aliens, and allow pregnancies to come almost to term and steal the fetuses. They often place implants into the abductees' bodies, for tracking or identification or maybe to merely mess with our minds. Some believe the entire phenomenon is entirely real but that its goal is psychiatric in nature.

Another interpretation is that the aliens are benevolent and extremely committed to the spiritual growth of the human race. If they tamper with our bodies, it is to set our physical plant aright so that we may tap into energies that will allow us to evolve to our next stage of being. The grays are angels, our angels—those angels—have always been angels, have been falsely identified over the millennia and only now are seen as our alien friends.

Conversely, researchers with a fundamentalist Christian bent call them demons, similarly misidentified over the centuries as vampires, succubi ... Satan.

Personally, I do not know if there is a Satan, but the grays will answer until he comes along. If the events reported have any truth at all, then the grays are evil incarnate.

There is no denying that those who claim to have been carried off by grays are tormented by their very real but uncertain memories, which their minds sometimes, but not always, force into the subconscious. (Contrary to popular belief, there are many abductees who recall the experience without hypnosis. Others recall the experiences in dreams.)

Many abductees are frightened and ashamed, coming forward with their stories only after careful deliberation. After much soul searching, for example, Whitley Strieber in 1987 wrote a book about his own abduction experiences, offering much-needed support to others who lived in denial and also popularizing what once was a dim and embarrassing corner of ufology. Until Strieber, very few stories of abductions were accepted by UFO researchers.

For Strieber, it all began in that out-of-the-way, long-neglected, soft and sleepy pastoral state that we call ... Wisconsin.

Strieber is a novelist, and his stories are often about the supernatural. He wrote *The Wolfen* and *The Hunger*. Some would say that his interest in UFOs and abduction stories is therefore suspicious. Strieber would argue, as he did in his 1987 book, *Communion*, that his fascination with the paranormal may have grown out of his repressed UFO experiences and not the other way around.

He has been abducted repeatedly, he said, beginning with a train trip from Madison in July 1957.

Strieber, his father and sister had flown up from their home in San Antonio, Texas, to visit an aunt and uncle. On their return, they took a train. While many of Strieber's memories are clouded, parts of the train trip are snapshot sharp—unusually sharp for his age at the time, which was 12.

While most of the trip took place at night, it seems that the UFO event occurred early, during the day, while the family was still in Wisconsin. Strieber recalls looking out at a countryside of thick pine woods. He remembers seeing above the landscape a "great hooked object floating in the air, which on closer inspection proved to be a triangle."

After that, something happened that he later recalled as a series of shapes, images that may only be symbolic of what his youthful mind experienced. One moment he was in the train, sitting up, awake, and the next he was sitting on a sort of bed with sides. It had a soft seat and solid arms. His movements were somehow restricted.

In front of him were rows of soldiers, dressed in fatigues, sprawled as if comatose. (Remember here that the nature of any given abduction's reality is unclear; it may be that the stories are only the mind's expression of experiences that are beyond comprehension. It's possible that the stories may be best understood as a symbolic recollection of a real event.) Anyway, the soldiers were on closed platforms whose sides canted slightly inward, from top to bottom. There was a yellow-brown creature with a floppy, lipless mouth and a copper-colored wand. Strieber and the being had a brief conversation, during which the creature explained the presence of the soldiers.

"We look them over and send them home," it said in a high, light voice.

Strieber remembered something being pushed down his throat. After a while, he saw his sister sprawled to the right. She was wearing her nightgown. Their father was four feet away, standing in his pajamas, making convulsive movements with his mouth, as if he were choking.

Strieber told his father, "Oh, Daddy! Daddy, don't be scared! Come on, Daddy. Daddy, it's all right!"

His father said, "Whitty, it's not all right! It's not all right!"

Then Strieber was on the train, and "I was sick as a dog," he recalled, "vomiting and vomiting up bile." The porter and a doctor, who was a passenger on the train, tried to help. The illness began in the middle of the night and continued until the next morning.

The sharpest memories of the entire trip center around the illness Strieber experienced after the abduction, which he only recalled years later, under hypnosis. The whole experience, Strieber later thought, was a psychological examination or experiment. That first visit, he believes, identified him to the visitors as one of their chosen ones, individuals who are repeatedly examined, decade after decade.

While Strieber's stories, by their very nature, are nearly beyond belief, in 1986 he took a lie-detector test to verify his story, as well as stories of subsequent abductions.

He passed it.

Strieber is certainly the most famous and most eloquent of the abductees. What follows is the text of a letter from a less eloquent man, whose experiences are even more bizarre. He has requested anonymity. I have edited his letter only slightly. I received it from a third party, a person who claims links with several intelligence agencies.

Dear Sir:

First off, I would like to make it very clear that we are not emotionally unstable people or that our experiences are a figment of our imagination, although I wish they were. It often bothers me when I hear people tell us that they wish they could have an experience like us. They have no idea what they are saying. They have no idea of the nightmares and the horror we went through. Personally, I enjoy watching sci-fi flicks on TV, and that is the scenerio that we prefer to see encounters in.

We have never had any hypnotism, or gone to any counseling. We kept it mainly to ourselves, out of fear of being harassed and mocked. Except for a few family members.

I was a trained office machine service technician, in the field for over 23 years. I was employed by such companies as Rockwell International Microelectronics Division as an electronics technician. I also owned my own office machine business at one time, before I became disabled. I am 49 years old.

My encounters began at the age of 6. I was visited one afternoon by a short, dark-robed being (robed from head to foot). I was unable to move, either due to fear, or [because] the being had some kind of hold on me. The being slowly inched its way up to my bed, within feet from my face. That's the last I remembered.

Many years later, in 1972, my wife and I saw a bright light in front of our car as we were driving down a country highway late one night. We stopped the car, as the light hovered above us. My wife and I leaned forward and peered at the metallic disc-shaped object that was about 50 feet above us. We could see the windows, colored lights and shape of the ship. There was no sound, no crickets, no wind, just total silence.

At first I was curious and in a state of awe. But then within an oddly short period of time, my feelings turned 180 degrees to that of intense fear, and a terrible feeling that I had to escape from THEM! We drove off at a high rate of speed. We arrived home over two to three hours later.

I realized we were missing time. We had gone to visit a police officer friend of mine, and had left his house at exactly 12 midnight (because the officer's shift on duty began at 12 midnight). The 15-mile stretch back to our town should have only taken about 20 to 25 minutes at the most, not two hours. My 1-year-old daughter and 2-year-old son were also in the car with us.

I am convinced that we were abducted by aliens. My son remembered many years later that he recalls seeing geometric shapes on a wall that night, but that is all we recall, except for the intense fear and terror, especially after we got home. Every time my wife talked about the episode, I felt like I was going to faint from terror. It was like something triggered off inside telling me to "shut up," "don't talk about it."

In the early 1980s, in Iron Ridge (Dodge County), Wis., my daughter had an encounter in our trailer home in the country where we lived. (We have often moved to remote country areas to live. We just love the solitude). My youngest daughter, who was about 8 or 10 years old at the time, told me several years later that one afternoon while she was down for a nap, she saw toys floating around the room. At first she thought they were kind of neat. Then she saw a large picture of a human's anatomy. Next she tells me she remembers a hand going inside of her and then pain! She can probably explain it in more detail than I can.

When she was older (after she was 16 and had not begun menstruating), she had a probe with a camera inserted next to her belly button to examine her internally. The doctors discovered that she had no reproductive organs. So what in the hell is going on? She has the medical records and findings of that examination. As parents, we know that she was intact as a child.

There were other occurrences in the 1980s where I had a long thin arm and hand grab me around my middle area to hold me in bed. I grabbed at the hand and threw it away. I was not asleep, I was awake, and it was not a dreamlike atmosphere. At the time, I was not on any drugs of any sort, or alcohol. I had been drinking at one time, but at that time it had been at least five years after I did drink. I just do not believe in alcohol.

My son and both my daughters recall many times seeing beings in their bedrooms since childhood. They attest to the fact that they were not dreams and insist to this day (they are now 19, 24 and 25 years old) that what they saw was real.

The 1991 abduction and encounters were the most strange and terrible of all. In order for me to explain it the best way, I must start from the beginning and try to put in order the sequence of events leading up to it.

We lived at that house where the events took place from May 1988 to Sept 1, 1992. The place was North Freedom (Sauk County), Wis., and again we lived in a very remote wilderness-type area, about 15 miles from the largest town, and 10 miles from a small town. The area was heavily wooded and had the highest hills in the state. We lived on one of the highest points.

In the summer of 1991, I had seen a large meteor-type fire-ball (greenish and green and orange flames and smoke) fall from the sky. It looked like it fell only five miles from where I could see it coming down. Other neighbors in the area saw it as well. It was an extraordinary sighting to say the least.

Also that summer, one night as I had just laid down for bed, I saw colored lights flashing across the window shade that was half down. The colored lights were coming from the outside. I jumped up and ran out of the house in the back yard, yelling "They're back! They're back!" I still don't know why I said that.

My wife got up and came outside, along with my children, I think. But the lights were gone. Then while we were either standing out back looking up at the sky or in the house looking out of a large window, we saw a patch of clouds, and behind these clouds were brightly flashing colored lights (large), flashing as the cloud patch moved to the east. No other clouds in the sky. It was a clear, warm summer's night. Again, it was the oddest thing we ever saw.

Now, getting closer to the December 1991 encounter we had. It was around the middle of December, and one night I was relaxing, watching a TV show, and it was about 8 p.m. My youngest daughter had just gone up the steps to bed. Within a matter of 10 minutes or so she came running down the steps and stood next to me shaking and breathless. I asked her why she hadn't gone to bed yet. All she could say was, "Dad! Dad! Do you hear it? Do you hear it?"

I replied, "Hear what?"

She said, "The rocket engine. Listen!" Then I heard it. The roar of an engine and the shaking of the house. I couldn't believe it. I asked her what was going on. She had told me that it was a space ship of some sort, and that it was outside just above her window. She said the lights were shining in the room (different colors) and she had just laid down and it began. She got up to look out the window, and there it was, the ship, maybe only 20 to 30 feet above the roof of the house, but sticking out far enough that she could see a large portion of it at the top of her window. She then turned in panic and ran screaming from the room down the steps. The rest I just mentioned.

I told my wife and older daughter, who were in the kitchen, and they too had felt something. My older daughter told me later that something was calling to her (mental telepathy, I think) to go outside, and she had an irresistible feeling that she had to go, but Mom wouldn't let her as she had to keep on her homework. This happened fairly much the same time that [the other daughter] saw the ship.

Within a half hour, I called the Sauk County Sheriff's Department and reported a UFO encounter. They took the information and told me that they were going to relay it to some other agency or agencies to investigate. They asked me about the sighting. After that phone call, the Sauk County Sheriff's Department called back and told me that a woman (unknown to us) called and reported seeing a UFO in her binoculars, and that it fairly much fit the description of what my daughter explained originally. The Sheriff's Department was totally convinced by then that something was going on.

Other reports came in from the nearby area of an alien ship hovering in a person's yard and then leaving and coming back to the same person's yard.

We also received a strange call from Washington. That's all I know of where the call came from. The caller wouldn't give me any more information than that he was watching this on radar, and had seen it over our house for over 30 minutes to an hour before it took off at a tremendous speed and went off the radar screen. He also reassured me that he believed me and that it was really happening to us. But he would not give me any more details of just exactly where he was from or who he was, except that he had been contacted. Very odd.

Over the next two to four weeks was a haze of fear of the unknown, with further visitations in and around the area where we lived. My son reported seeing a field being lit up with a powerful light, as if being searched and scanned. My daughter and I saw the same thing one night while taking a drive to Baraboo. We saw this funnel-type light that scanned this field and house.

There were several nights that, late at night, I could hear footsteps going up the stairs, walking around upstairs. I was terrified. Finally, after several nights of this, it seemed I was able to get up the courage to grab my assault weapon that I had especially prepared with a fully loaded 30-round clip with full metal jacket M-16 loads in it.*

I was on the edge of losing it at that time. I searched the rooms and found nothing.

I just came to a place where I became so exhausted by the seemingly nightly visits of those beings that I kind of just

---

* Author's note: I don't recommend this course of action. For one thing, it probably won't do you any good. In a well-documented 1955 encounter at Hopkinsville, Ky., similar night visitors easily survived point-blank shotgun blasts. For another thing, even if the abduction experience is actual, it is clear that the percipient's reality during the encounter is highly subjective. Familiar objects and people may appear unfamiliar. Guns are not a good idea.

resolved myself to accept the situation and pray for them to leave us and go.

My son woke one of those mornings without any clothes on at all. He told me that he couldn't explain that, and he was quite shaken up over the situation. My daughters also reported other things I cannot remember at this time. It seemed like the encounters went on for well over a month, maybe longer. We were all worn out and psyched out, and I truly thought I had had it mentally.

My wife and I examined our [younger] daughter, [and we] had my older daughter examine the younger one, too. We were again shocked. Her female parts had been removed, just as with our older daughter. We all know for a fact that she was intact before this. In fact, one year before, after my oldest daughter got back her latest examination reports and confirmed that she had parts missing, we examined our youngest. She was normal. And like I said, one year later, it's all changed.

Dr. P. (our family doctor) examined both daughters in 1992 or '93 for a school physical. He was shocked at his findings. I was approached by him [to see] if my girls had had surgery. I told him no, and he persisted in getting to the bottom of it. I knew I had no other choice but to tell him the crazy story. And I was sure he would think I was a madman. Well, he believed me and was convinced from what he saw that something extraordinary had happened to them. Dr. P. said he would be happy to submit his findings from the examination.

We had moved from that house where the encounters had happened in September 1992, primarily to get away from there for fear of it happening again with the encounters. I have realized that I know they have followed me since my youth, and now are following me with my family. But we had to move anyway.

We moved to Algoma (Kewaunee County), Wis. We had one experience when we lived in a trailer temporarily until we could get a house. Two bright red orbs came straight down in back of our trailer one night. (My youngest daughter was home alone when this happened.) She told me the family dog went nuts and started barking and warned her. Then she looked out the window and saw the two red orbs or spheres land in the field and disappear. When I came home, I quickly grabbed my video camera and went for a search. Nothing was found.

Several months later, all of us (my son and two daughters) were visited, we believe, by aliens, one night. We all spoke to one another the next morning, unknowing what had happened to each other the night before. I reported hearing footsteps in the hall. My son felt like someone was in his room and he could not sleep. My two daughters felt the same way as my son. We believe that they came back to check up on us. Since that time, we have had no further contacts.

We had stayed in the closet for a long time with our story because of fear of being treated like crazy people. I have been telling our encounters to some people in the past few years, but so many people mock it and treat us terrible. We are so sick of that. After seeing my last daughter abducted and left sterile by aliens, I just couldn't keep quiet any longer. It's TRUE! It happened.

God help those who have and are going through what we have gone through.

"ONE OF OUR
F-89s IS DOWN"

On the night of Nov. 23, 1953, a Madison-based U.S. Air Force plane pursued a UFO over Lake Superior. Observers tracking the plane on a radarscope saw it merge with the UFO. The plane was never heard from again. No wreckage has ever been found.

It was an F-89C, Serial No. 51-5853A, assigned to the 433rd Fighter-Interceptor Squadron in Madison. The plane temporarily had been loaned to Kinross Air Force Base, near Saulte St. Marie, and had been sent aloft to take part in an Active Air Defense Mission.

After the plane disappeared, the ground control intercept officer at Kinross notified the public information officer at Madison's Truax Field of the incident.

"One of our F-89s is down," the Kinross officer said. "It went after an unknown. This thing showed up on radar over the Soo locks, then headed over Lake Superior. Our jet zeroed in on this object at 500 miles per hour. We watched the blips on the scope. The two blips merged. Then there was nothing. We've been unable to establish radio contact with the plane and presume it's lost."

The plane was lost shortly after 1851 Eastern Standard Time and was about 150 miles northeast of Kinross, over northern Lake Superior, when it went down. From the official crash report summary: "The radar return from the other aircraft [the UFO] indicated it was continuing on its original flight path, while the return from the F-89 disappeared."

Nothing was ever found of the plane's two occupants: 26-year-old Lt. Felix Moncla Jr., who was the pilot; and 22-year-old Lt. Robert L. Wilson, who was the radar observer. That's the first mystery.

The second concerns the way the U.S. Air Force handled the matter.

The U.S. Air Force maintained, according to the crash report summary, that "The unknown aircraft being intercepted was a Royal Canadian Air Force Dakota (C-47), Serial No. VC-912, flying from Winnipeg to Sudbury, Canada. At the time of the interception, it was crossing northern Lake Superior from west to east at 7,000 feet," the exact height at which the F-89 had been flying.

The Royal Canadian Air Force countered by saying that was a lie.

"The C-47 was traveling on a flight plan taking it over Canadian territory; this alone would seem to make such an intercept unlikely," wrote W.B. Totman, squadron leader and acting director of public relations for the Royal Canadian Air Force, in 1953. Furthermore, "a check of RCAF records has revealed no report of an incident involving an RCAF aircraft in the Lake Superior area on the above date."

The Truax public information office gave the UFO version of the story to the Associated Press. The news organization in turn began distributing the story to its member newspapers. The story ran in an early edition of the *Chicago Tribune*.

It did not appear in later editions.

Maj. Donald E. Keyhoe, a retired Marine Corps officer-turned UFO investigator, intimated in 1957 that the story was suppressed at the request of the military. "The Air Force should tell us the results of their investigation," Keyhoe said. "What was the unknown? I say that the evidence points to a midair collision between the F-89 and something else. What was that object? Where did it come from?"

Keyhoe was controversial but he was no kook. Earlier, Albert Chop, a U.S. Air Force press officer, had even written Keyhoe a letter of recommendation: "We in the Air Force recognize Maj. Keyhoe as a responsible, accurate reporter. His long association and cooperation with the Air Force, in our study of unidentified flying objects, qualifies him as a leading civilian authority."

The U.S. Air Force subsequently theorized that "the pilot probably suffered from vertigo and crashed into the lake." However, given the weather and time of day, it is far more likely that the pilot would have been flying on instruments at the time. That's why pilots fly on instruments in the first place—to fly when their own senses can't be trusted. Vertigo could not have affected his flight. Furthermore, his radar observer would have been watching instruments as the distance between the F-89 and the intruder closed.

Arthur Caperton, a senior crash investigator with the civilian Civil Aeronautics Board, called the Air Force's changing explanations "idiotic."

"Who are they trying to kid?" he said. He wanted to see transcripts of the radio communications between plane and ground control—which have never been released. Caperton suspected that there were additional details that were kept secret.

"Put yourself in Moncla's place," he said. "You're closing in on the thing. The last few seconds you see something—maybe you suddenly know what's behind all this. Wouldn't you yell it into your throat microphone? ... You'd instinctively yell something, and ground control would hear it."

When the Madison *Capital Times* investigated Keyhoe's charges in 1957, a U.S. Air Force press officer responded, "Don't get your readers all steamed up about these things. It will only mean that we'll start getting a flood of sightings from Wisconsin that will cost the Air Force a lot of the taxpayers' money to investigate."

But wasn't the death of two Air Force officers worth the attention that Keyhoe urged?

"Lots of atmospheric conditions cause blips on radar," said the U.S. Air Force spokesman. "And lots of planes go down."

... Lots of planes go down?

THE 1975 UFO WAVE

"It was flashing," said Ashland County Undersheriff George Ree. "I say it was green and white. The deputies claim it was blue and white, so maybe I'm color blind. I do not know. I still say it was green and white instead of blue and white. I'll go along with their story. There's more of them than me."

Ree was talking to Alan Landsburg, producer of the television series "In Search Of," about the strange events in and around Mellen, about 20 miles south of Ashland, the night of March 13, 1975.

Although Landsburg's re-creation of the event for his 1970s television show, narrated by Leonard Nimoy, was dramatic, it was also too tame. Landsburg re-created a single event. In reality, authorities in four northern counties reported UFO sightings that night, kicking off the all-time greatest wave of reports in the state. Over time the wave covered 40 Wisconsin counties.

The first night was strange enough. Police told the Associated Press that the UFOs garbled or totally jammed their radio messages. Civilian witnesses in Ashland, Douglas, Iron and Pierce counties saw the objects move, change color and head toward what seemed to be a common point in the sky. No radar contact was made at the nearby Duluth, Minn., airport.

The incidents began at the home of Phil Baker, his wife and four children, in rural Mellen. He was a machine operator at the Seaway Division of Louisiana Pacific, which produced high-grade wood veneer. At around 9 p.m., Baker was inside when his 15-year-old daughter, Jane, decided to put the cats outside. From the yard, she saw a dome-shaped object with a brilliant halo sitting on the road.

"I felt like running," Jane said. "I didn't know where to go. I got really scared, so I ran into the house." She told her father about the object, and the two went outside together.

"Bluish-green lights and red lights were around the outside, and in the center it had a real brilliant yellowish-green light that appeared to be coming from inside," Phil Baker said. "It was really brilliant, and when I looked at it I kind of had to squint my eyes.

"The object was making a very loud, high-pitched whiny sound. As we watched it, the high-pitched noise died down. ... The red and green lights—they dimmed until the colored lights went out completely. The halo that appeared to be over it also dimmed considerably. And then it made a noise. It was like heavy metal hammering."

Baker was frightened, but he thought he should move closer. By this time, his wife had come outside, though she would not leave the porch. She yelled for him to leave the object alone. They called Undersheriff Ree, "and when I was on the telephone speaking to him," Baker said, "the lights on the object faded off and there was a bang, and it disappeared, and that was the end of the object." Ree came out anyway and calmed the family. Since there was no evidence to back up the story, Baker urged Ree to keep the incident secret. Fearing ridicule, the entire family agreed that they must not tell anyone else of the sighting. Others, however, were already confirming their story.

"Telephones were ringing off the hook from citizens who saw the object," said Ashland County Sheriff Joe Croteay. He asked Ree to meet Iron County deputies who were viewing a large, bright light nearby, just off Highway 77. Ree went out and met the officers, as well as one of his own deputies, at the site.

As the six officers clustered to watch the large white light, another light approached. "It was about at treetop level, traveling at a higher rate of speed toward that big bright light we had seen," Ree said. "The smaller light did not get too close to the large bright light."

Two more deputies were ordered, via radio, to travel 16 miles east of Ashland to a tower near Highway 2, west of Odanah, to see if a different view of the objects could offer additional information. Another light had since joined the first two. The second team of officers reported that the second light was the lowest of the three. It was flashing blue and white or green and white. The first light remained stationary, but the second was circling. The deputies later said it was dancing a jig.

"It was moving from left to right and was just having a good old time up there," Ree said.

Two of the lights were south of the highway and the third was north. After 15 to 30 minutes, the third light began to move. Ree radioed the officers at the tower that the light was approaching them. One of the officers had just returned to his squad car on Madigan Road when the light passed directly over him.

"His radio went out, and later—in about 30 seconds, 45 seconds—his radio came back on," Ree said. "He told us over the radio that the light was so bright he could have read a newspaper as this object went over his squad car."

The next night, Charles Larson of Madison said he and his wife used binoculars to watch a strange object for about a half hour, around 9 p.m. The sighting occurred near their home on Old Sauk Road. The Larsons said the object looked like "two plates held together, with one inverted over the other," with a row of lights along the edge.

Less than a month later the State Patrol communications center received reports from across the state of a bright blue-orange object that cut a swath across Wisconsin from Superior to Kenosha. The night of April 3, law enforcement officers and civilians in 40 counties reported the object, which did not appear on radar screens.

Three nights later, in Maiden Rock, in west-central Wisconsin, Donna Koehler looked out her bedroom window and saw lights inside and outside her neighbors' house, despite the fact that her neighbors had no yard light and were away from home.

Koehler and her husband, Jim, discovered that the light came from a bright orange object in the sky. "At times it kind of switched colors and twinkled green and blue and red and white," she said. "Every time I'd turn off the lights it would move in closer to us. Then when we turned them back on, it would back off."

After calling the police, the two fled their home.

"The minute we got in the car we took off [and the] light bounced just almost over the top of us and down in these little gullies we live in," she said. "I hollered at my husband. And then we kept going and it came up again and I hollered and it landed in the field. I looked out and there's this great big glow of orange."

United Press International reported that the sighting coincided with several others that night. In Elmwood, in northern Wisconsin, police officer George Wheeler saw a huge ball of flame come over a hill from the northeast. At first he thought it was an airliner about to crash.

"It was cigar-shaped, kind of orange, with blue flashes," he said. The UFO's flames lit up the horizon as Wheeler followed it down a country road. The object was the size of a football field. Wheeler drove into a ditch when it seemed that the object was about to crash, but instead it hovered over him. There was no sound.

The object then flew toward the south, and Wheeler again followed it, this time to a pasture where it hovered about 1,500 feet above the ground. It was around 11 p.m., but the sky was bright. After some "aerobatics"—he later compared the movements to those of a joyriding pilot—the UFO flew away, to the west.

Wheeler said he could not wait to see a UFO again. Later, we'll find out that he did, with tragic results.

BELLEVILLE & ELMWOOD: THE UFO CAPITALS OF THE WORLD

As described in the preceding chapter, Elmwood police officer George Wheeler saw his first UFO in 1975. "I'm dying to get another chance at seeing one," he said.

Wheeler would get that wish.

And he would pay that price. Wheeler believed that the second UFO he saw killed him.

George Wheeler's Elmwood is one of two Wisconsin communities that calls itself the UFO Capital of the World, but, as we'll see later, only this northwestern Wisconsin town has the CIA stamp of approval. CIA agents came to investigate the town, along with Wheeler and his medical records. And perhaps to have a "UFO burger," as I have, at the village's annual UFO Days.

In Elmwood, UFOs are part of the summer scene. During the town's annual three-day July celebration, there are street dances, horseshoe tournaments, sidewalk sales, the coronation of a UFO Days queen, and food tents featuring UFO burgers. There's also a cow-chip throwing contest. When I attended, I bought the UFO Capital of the World T-shirt, UFO-Capital buttons, a UFO-Capital baseball cap and a

UFO-Capital bumper sticker. I bought the UFO shot glass with the city's crest (a sun setting behind a flying saucer), and the town's coffee mug (cow, barn, UFO). I had the UFO burger, which seemed much like an Earthly burger except for the sauerkraut. I searched in vain for the UFO medallion hidden somewhere in town (not a difficult task—you could jog the village's perimeter and not break a sweat). I did find an alien—green, stuffed and homemade. It had googly eyes and feelers, and on its chest was written "UFO DAYS." From a strange street vendor I bought a tiny piece of meat inside a tiny hermetically sealed vial. He claimed it was a piece of alien tissue from Roswell, N.M.

I also saw the squad car that George Wheeler was in when he was struck by a UFO's beam, which apparently burned out the car's plugs and points and gave Wheeler a fatal dose of radiation. I took a close-up picture of it. The people near me thought I was a little odd.

Obviously, alien visitation is an excuse for good-natured fun in Elmwood. It's also business, and it was to have been bigger business. In 1988 plans were announced for a $25 million visitors' center—for aliens. The UFO landing facility was to feature a complex array of lighting that would serve as a gigantic beacon, and a huge ground image of an alien and human meeting. The complex was to have covered 2 square miles, complete with housing for an international community of 50 to 100 scientists, along with sophisticated laboratories, a dining hall, a video studio and recreational facilities. About 200 people would have been employed, including maintenance and security personnel. Said Mayor Larry Feiler at the time, "This is not a gimmick."

The plan was actually pretty solid, as UFO landing strips go; all the Elmwood elements had, in fact, been earlier sketched out by Donald Keyhoe of NICAP. The Elmwood office for the landing center project received tens of thousands of letters, but, unfortunately, only $20,000. In 1990 the office was closed, though tired promoters held out hope that others would come forward and carry on. If nothing else, Elmwood had firmly established its earnestness in claiming to be the UFO Capital of the World.

Another UFO Capital of the World is the village of Belleville, which celebrates its UFO Day, complete with a parade, costume ball and other activities, each fall. I have been to this festival, too, and have seen the billboard at town's edge, the one that depicts Earth, an arrow pointing to the general vicinity of Belleville, and the legend "YOU ARE HERE." I bought the UFO-Capital postcard and saw the cheese shop and its signs announcing "Moon cheese (Swiss), \$2.50/lb." and "Out-of-this-world selection—imported cheese from the moon, Mars, Venus, Jupiter, Saturn, even Pluto!" I looked for but couldn't find a T-shirt. I took pictures again, and was again stared at.

In the case of both Elmwood and Belleville, the town's reputation as the UFO Capital of the World is deserved on the basis of enthusiasm alone. Neither town has had a lot of sightings within city limits, but both are definitely centered within larger areas of

The so-called "Belleville belt" of UFO activity is a distinct area of unexplained phenomena. Researchers refer to these areas as "windows."

high UFO activity. However, in attracting tourists, each town stakes its claim primarily on the basis of a single high-profile sighting. In both cases, police officers were witnesses.

On Jan. 15, 1987, Belleville police officer Glen Kazmar got the UFO flap rolling when he saw a clump of red, white and blue lights, "five or 20 times brighter than a normal star," hovering over the town. At 2:50 a.m., six hours after the sighting, he and a civilian "ride-along" spotted the lights again from a high point on Quarry Road, about three miles west of town. "It was very strange," Kazmar said. "I've been on the force over 10 years and been camping most of my life and I've never seen anything like it."

The Federal Aviation Administration was notified by the local police dispatcher. Milwaukee's Mitchell Field could not pick up the object, though Chicago radar reported a slow-moving contact. Radar in Aurora, Ill., also reported contact with the object. The UFO did not respond to radioed queries.

Sheriff's deputies in Dane and Green counties saw the object at the same time as Kazmar's second sighting. One of the Green County officers was in Albany, and the other was a mile west.

By 3 a.m. four police cars were stationed on Quarry Road to observe the object. At 3:20 it started to move southwest. Kazmar followed it to Monticello. It dropped lower in the sky, picked up speed, then headed west.

"To be honest, I don't know what to think," Kazmar told the *Cap-*

ital Times in Madison. "In my line of work you try to keep an open mind about things."

Between Jan. 15 and March 21, about two dozen similar sightings were reported to the Chicago-based Center for UFO Studies, according to center co-director Don Schmitt. He said, however, that the most reliable sightings came the first night.

A subsequent incident occurred on March 8, 1987. At dusk, Lavonne Freidig and her son, Bill, saw a cigar-shaped object hang motionless for a period of time over a wooded area behind her home. It then departed, leaving a vapor trail and several smaller objects behind it. It was silhouetted against a red sunset. She told the Associated Press that her son, a freshman at the University of Wisconsin-Platteville, at first thought the object was a flock of geese.

But "the more I thought about it the more I thought, there's no way it could have been geese," Bill later said. Whatever it was, "it was really strange," said Lavonne Freidig, aide to state Sen. Lloyd Kincaid.

Belleville residents Harvey Funseth and Fred Gochenauer, while driving south on Highway 69, also saw an object that evening. It had a flashing light and was illuminated against the clouds. They stopped the car and got out, and Funseth, an employee of the state Department of Transportation, photographed the object several times with his 35-millimeter camera.

A billboard in Belleville welcomes alien visitors to the "UFO Capital of the World." Elmwood, Wis., also claims that status.

"Every one was a blank," he later said.

These are the sightings reported to the press, upon which Belleville's reputation as the UFO Capital of the World was built. After investigation, Schmitt of the Center for UFO Studies, who reviewed other reports, said the Belleville flap may have been more significant and less local than many believed. (Schmitt is one of the controversial researchers primarily responsible for the investigation of an alleged crashed flying saucer near Roswell, N.M., in 1947.)

Actually, the center of the UFO action was New Glarus, Schmitt said at a Belleville public forum. "It just happened that most of the witnesses were near Belleville when the UFOs were sighted." The sightings started in mid-January and lasted until mid-March.

Similarly, the Elmwood activity extended into the surrounding countryside, as shown in the previous chapter. Unexplained phenomena do seem to occur in geographical clusters (called "windows" in the trade). Why, no one knows.

It was the misfortune of Elmwood police officer George Wheeler to patrol that "window." A veteran of 30 years of policing, including 10 years as a New York State highway patrolman, Wheeler had never before taken UFOs seriously. But his second encounter was to prove very serious, indeed. Because of what happened to Wheeler the night of April 22, 1976, we must turn to the account made by Elmwood Police Chief Gene Helmer.

According to Helmer, at 11 p.m. Wheeler radioed that he was heading to the quarry, as it looked as if there was a fire there.

Wheeler approached the quarry from County P near Tuttle Hill. He radioed, "My God, it's one of those UFOs again." He started describing it very calmly: a silver oval with an orange-white dome, an electric-blue band girdling its center. In that band were portholes, or windows, and a block of horizontal lines that resembled fins. The object also had landing legs, and a lowered black hose or tube hanging from the bottom of it.

Then the radio went dead. The chief was listening from his part-time job at a nursing home. The nursing home's administrator, Paul Frederickson, lived right by the quarry. He was phoned.

"I got up and looked out the window and saw this flaming orange object in the sky," said Frederickson. "I watched it for a full 10 seconds and went back to bed to get my wife, but when we returned it was gone."

At the same time, a few miles away, Mrs. Miles Wergland's TV went out. She stood up and noticed a light outside. It was moving. "It was shaped like the moon but was much brighter and colored differently," she said. Later, it was found that televisions in three neighboring homes went off for 10 minutes, right when Wheeler's radio went dead. When the object left, Wergland's TV came back on.

David Moots, who was home babysitting, looked out the window and saw Wheeler's squad car sitting in the middle of the road. Moots went up to the car and found George Wheeler sprawled on the seat. Moots asked Wheeler if he was all right. Wheeler didn't answer. Moots asked again. Wheeler was barely conscious. He finally mumbled, "I've been hit. Get me to a radio."

Moots asked, "By a car?"

"No. By one of those UFOs."

The car's lights and ignition were off. Moots tried starting the car. It would not start. Later, it did start and was removed. Two days later, though, the car's spark plugs and points were found to be ruined.

Wheeler, still in a daze, was taken to Dr. Frank Springer and examined. Then he was taken home and was met by Chief Helmer, to whom he told his story. Wheeler was shaking all over. "Later, he didn't even

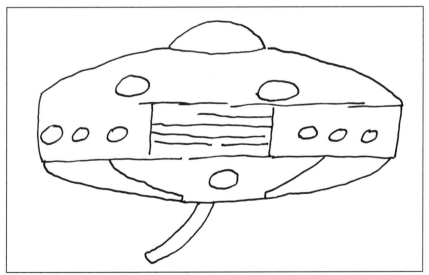

Before he died, Elmwood police officer George Wheeler drew a picture of the UFO that he believed killed him. Redrawn for reproduction here, the strange craft struck Wheeler's squad car with a beam of light, knocking out the officer and ruining the engine's spark plugs. (Courtesy of the Eau Claire Leader-Telegram)

remember describing the incident to me," Helmer said.

What had happened was this: Wheeler came up on the road overlooking the quarry. The object was hovering. He could see a vertical paddle-wheel motion on one side. He observed shadow figures inside. The object was 250 feet wide and 2 stories high. It shot out a bluish-white light, which struck Wheeler.

Wheeler subsequently was hospitalized in Menomonie. Then he was moved to a hospital in Eau Claire for 11 days of testing. Then he was moved back to Menomonie. From his hospital bed in Memorial Hospital, Wheeler told the *Eau Claire Leader Telegram* that UFOs "are not harmless but, in fact, they're out to kill us."

He did not feel well. He had pain in his arms and legs, and unbearable headaches. "Nobody seems to be able to determine what my ailment is," he said. "I'm reluctant to say it, but I think it is possible I got a good dose of radiation from that UFO."

He died six months later. There was no autopsy, but Dr. Springer believed he may have suffered a heart attack.

The CIA would investigate.

Hard to believe? We'll find proof of their investigation—and its results—next.

THE MEN IN BLACK

"If the Air Force said there was such a thing as flying saucers, don't you believe them. If they said there is no such thing as flying saucers, don't you believe them. If they said I don't know what I was talking about, don't you believe them. In brief, don't believe them. Believe me."

—Frank Scully, *Behind the Flying Saucers*

Frank Scully was one of the first UFO researchers to suggest that the government had secretly recovered crashed flying saucers. In fact, one of his investigations involved a disc that had been seen flying over Black River Falls, Wis. An electrician found the small craft lying in some deep grass in the Jackson County fairgrounds and exhibited it in a sideshow. Local police confiscated the UFO and stored it in a bank vault, then sent it to Milwaukee's Mitchell Field, where it was studied by aircraft experts. Examination showed that the disc was made of plywood.

"This contrivance is patently a hoax," said officials. "It will be held for a reasonable time and then disposed of in the nearest ash receptacle."

But Scully had other, better stories of recovered UFOs, and from them he popularized the theory that the government knows far more than it is saying about UFOs. So pervasive has this belief become that a 1995 survey conducted by the Scripps Howard News Service revealed that 50 percent of U.S. citizens believe that UFOs exist and that the federal government is covering up what it knows.

The conspiracy theory was brought to life early on by Wisconsinite Ray Palmer. Palmer, as I mentioned earlier in this book, was the pulp-magazine publisher who believed that an evil race of robots, named Deros, lived far beneath the surface of the earth. Whatever you think of Palmer's theories, there's no denying the impact he made on the public in terms of its acceptance of flying saucers. In the early years, before anyone else took the phenomenon seriously, Palmer persisted, sketching the agenda for almost all the debate that would follow.

Whatever UFOs are, the way we perceive them is largely due to Palmer. In *Amazing Stories* and *Fantastic Adventures* magazines, he launched the modern myth of the flying saucer. He was the original UFO buff. In the 1950s he moved his offices from Chicago to Amherst, Wis., where he continued to publish UFO publications for an ever smaller audience.

Palmer's career waned as "flying saucers" gave way to the more properly named "UFO." His enthusiasm and willingness to believe even the craziest stories became embarrassing to more scholarly researchers. Despite his impact on the field, Palmer was an obscure figure at the time of his death, in 1977, and he is more obscure now.

Why? In one of Palmer's magazines, *Forum*, he theorized that there was "an organized something that goes into action when people like myself seem to be on the verge of being successful in their goals, and [it] effectively smashes everything to bits."

That may have been sour grapes on Palmer's part, but it is a fact that every once in a while someone surfaces to put a chill into someone else's interest in UFOs. Collectively, these people are known in the field as the Men in Black (or MIBs, for short) since they usually dress in black. Sometimes, though, they wear uniforms and even display military IDs. Even the Air Force, which could not believe in UFOs, believed in the MIBs.

From a March 1, 1967, memo from the Air Force assistant vice chief of staff, Lt. General Hewitt T. Wheless, distributed throughout the service:

"Information, not verifiable, has reached Headquarters USAF that persons claiming to represent the Air Force or other Defense establishments have contacted citizens who have sighted unidentified flying objects. In one reported case an individual in civilian clothes, who represented himself as a member of NORAD (North American Air Defense Command), demanded and received photos belonging to a private citizen. In another, a person in an Air Force uniform approached local police and other citizens who had sighted a UFO, assembled them in a school room and told them they did not see what they thought they saw and that they should not talk to anyone about the sighting."

Wheless advised, "All military and civilian personnel and particularly Information Officers and UFO Investigating Officers who hear of such reports should immediately notify their local OSI (USAF Office of Special Investigations) offices."

There are very few classic MIB stories, complete with black suits, but there are many MIB-like tales. The stereotypical Man in Black shows up at your door, having driven there in a large black car, usually an American model, usually older, and always in perfect condition. The Man in Black is dressed just that way, like a Cold War spy. He will appear vaguely Asian, be somewhat pale, and have what seems like a foreigner's grasp of the language. Typically, he will argue that you did not see what you thought you saw. If you persist in your belief, he will threaten your life.

For conspiracy buffs, the MIBs are a treat. Are they aliens? Government agents? CIA? FBI? It's a silly sideshow on the fringe of a fringe science.

Until it happens to you. Then it's not quite so funny.

In 1991, I wrote a newspaper story about a man who was using the Freedom of Information Act to obtain the release of UFO documents from the National Security Agency. At the time, I was a free-lance columnist and critic for the *Capital Times* in Madison. For some years, to avoid late-night crank calls, my phone number had been unlisted. Naturally, the paper was happy to take messages, but it was a strict rule that staff did not give out the home phone numbers or addresses of any of its reporters—to the displeasure of old schoolmates who sometimes tried to look me up.

But after my Freedom of Information Act story ran, I got a call at home from a man named George. George said he had enjoyed the article very much. He thought that it was time people were told the truth, he said. Unfortunately, though, he had relatives who worked for the CIA. George wanted to warn me that if I persisted in this line of investigation, I would find that it took longer to receive my mail. It would be diverted, opened, read, resealed and sent on its way. Also, my phone might be tapped. But George wished me success.

I didn't quite know what to say. I thanked him and that was that.

His "gratitude" was not comforting, however, but distressing—an effect he probably desired. I immediately wondered ... how had George gotten my unlisted phone number? I checked with my editors, but they had not given it out. They had not even been asked for it. No one had called the newspaper for me.

In the summer of 1996, as I prepared this book, I came home one night and was told by my housemates that I'd just missed a visitor. It was a man, a sort of odd man. He had asked for me by describing me in pretty vague terms. "He interviews people," was what the man said. He left his name.

His name was George.

George is my Man in Black.

George may not work for the government, but he has colleagues who have. From Jan. 14 through 18, 1953, there convened a CIA panel subsequently referred to as the Robertson committee. Its existence was long denied, as was the purpose for its formation: the UFO problem.

In its final report, declassified in 1967, the panel said it "took cognizance of the existence of such groups as the 'Civilian Flying Saucer Investigators' (Los Angeles) and the 'Aerial Phenomena Research Organization' (Wisconsin). It was believed that such organizations should be watched because of their potentially great influence on mass thinking if widespread sightings should occur. The apparent irresponsibility and possible use of such groups for subversive purposes should be kept in mind."

The Wisconsin private-interest group referred to in the report is the now-defunct APRO, founded by the late Jim and Coral Lorenzen. They established APRO in Green Bay and subsequently moved operations to Tucson, Ariz. It was an early, pioneering group, and why anyone should believe it would pose a threat is somewhat odd. When the Robertson panel met, APRO was just a year old.

In 1952, during APRO's first summer—even before the CIA panel recommended surveillance—the Lorenzens lived on Memorial Drive in Green Bay. One day, two men drove up their street, slowly, as if looking for a specific house. They chose to call on the Lorenzens. One of the men explained that they were house painters. They would like to offer a bid.

The Lorenzens were only renting the house in which they lived. They could not authorize a painting contract. The man was content to engage Coral in conversation. He never did remember to ask for the landlord's name. After the two "house painters" left, they continued down the street, turned the corner, went around the block—and waited in their car. Coral watched them from the back of her house. Presumably, they watched her, too. No other homes in the immediate neighborhood were canvassed. Coincidentally, other local APRO members that same day were also visited by painting contractors. In no case did the painters work very hard to actually gain any clients. They were just happy to ... talk.

Recalled Coral, years later, "Perhaps they were painting contractors, but if so, they certainly were not very enterprising ones."

The Lorenzens did have one particular associate who showed a great deal of enterprise, however. "One of our first, most energetic supporters was a gentleman from Green Bay," Coral recalled in one of her several books, *UFOs Over the Americas*. "He helped with minor donations and many suggestions for the organization. He claimed to have a background in intelligence work."

Among his other talents, this man was a careful typist who used platens. Readers who learned to type before word processing will remember that a platen is a second sheet of paper you put in the typewriter so that the keys won't score the roller. The platen acts as a buffer, to dampen the impact of the keys.

The Lorenzen's benefactor wrote to them on Feb. 22, 1953. He had the misfortune to write his letter on a sheet of paper he had previously used as a platen. Coral Lorenzen noticed the barely visible impressions on the back of the letter after she had tossed it into a wastebasket. She shaded the paper with a soft pencil and was surprised to find herself reading a history of her residences, a list of her personal habits, and conclusions regarding her character.

The Lorenzens asked their "friend" about this, and he stated, according to Coral, "that this was merely a routine he used to formulate his feelings about people he met and to define his own impressions and that it was strictly a report for his own files."

The Lorenzens didn't know what to believe, and felt that his explanation could be genuine. (For my part, I believe that the Lorenzens' optimistic assessment is the first solid evidence we have for the influence of the thought ray belonging to the evil Deros civilization.)

In a separate incident, a couple of less pleasant MIBs broke into a Madison hotel room. Sometime in the 1970s, free-lance journalist Warren Smith came to Madison to check out a UFO sighting. A farmer had seen a UFO in his orchard. (This is probably the 1968 Stoughton sighting because that would put the event near Madison and because that was the sighting during which the UFO gave out a shower of sparks, suggesting a litter of debris.) The incident was also reported to a law enforcement agency, which, as it turns out, is a prerequisite for the later involvement by the Men in Black.

Anyway, Smith came to Madison and checked into a Holiday Inn. He made arrangements to visit the farmer and found that the man had recovered a piece of metal, apparently from the UFO. The farmer gave the metal to Smith. Smith came back to Madison. Then the farmer spoke with Smith again and said that a fertilizer salesman had been out, asking a lot about the UFO and the metal but not working too hard to sell fertilizer. The farmer needed to see Smith again.

No stranger to the paranoia of ufology, Smith took the back off the TV in his hotel room and tied the metal sample to the inside. "I asked the maids and hotel maintenance man to watch my room during my absence," Smith told British UFO researcher Timothy Good, as recounted in Good's book, *Above Top Secret*.

As soon as Smith left, two men with a room key went in. A maid saw it all and went in a minute later, pretending to check the room. She saw the two going through Smith's suitcase.

Meanwhile, Smith was talking to the farmer, who had since met with some representatives from the government who wanted the metal. The farmer had agreed, he said, based on "national security, a danger to the world, and the government's desire."

Well, Smith went back to Madison, back to the hotel, back to his room, and there encountered his two visitors. One was at the desk; the other was stretched out on the bed. One of the men said, "You have something we want. A farmer gave you a piece of metal the other day. Our job is to pick it up."

Smith asked to see some identification.

"Name the agency and we'll produce it," the man said. "Would you like Air Force, FBI, or maybe NORAD [North American Aerospace Defense Command]?"

Smith was growing increasingly uncomfortable. He had only been loaned the metal. The farmer wanted it to go to the government. Smith agreed to turn over the fragment if the men would answer a few questions. They agreed, and all adjourned to the hotel coffee shop. There, of course, the men didn't really offer any information, other than that "UFOs involve more than you or any civilian can realize. They're the most important thing and perhaps the greatest hazard that mankind has ever faced."

Smith turned over the metal and saw the men off. Their car had Illinois plates. He immediately called Brad Steiger, a well-known paranormal investigator who resides in Iowa. Some years afterward, Steiger recalled that Smith sounded "genuinely frightened" about the event.

Smith said later that he traced the plates to a Chicago man with "CIA links," after which Smith apparently went underground, as he cannot be located today.

If Chicago is the base of operations for Midwestern MIBs, I believe the activity is centered in that city's Great Lakes Naval Base. There is anecdotal evidence that UFO debris is brought there. In 1973 a gunners mate, recruited by Naval Intelligence, was stationed at the base. He was given a high security clearance and was promised an even higher clearance and an overseas assignment if he performed well for the next year and a half.

"Now, I was sequestered one night for guard duty on a Quonset hut at the northwestern end of the base," the gunners mate told Lawrence Fawcett and Barry J. Greenwood, researchers who have made extensive use of the Freedom of Information Act to gain government documents relating to UFOs. "We were told there was highly top secret material in that Quonset hut. We were not supposed to go inside and not to look in any windows. We were to guard the place and let no one in or out without the proper identification."

However, this one night the gunners mate was officer of the guard, and a messenger brought him a letter to be given to the officer on duty. It was for the officer on duty's eyes only, and the gunners mate had to get a signature on the front of the sealed envelope. He had to go inside.

He called and explained, and as the officer on duty was busy just at that moment, it was decided to let the gunners mate enter the Quonset hut. "Now this was highly unusual," the gunners mate recalled. He took it to be a test of his discretion.

He went through the large metal sliding door, signed in, and then walked down the hallway, escorted by three officers. He took a turn to the right, walked five feet, went about eight feet down another hallway, turned left for five more feet, and walked into a warehousing area, "where I saw a strange craft off to my left."

"The craft was possibly 30 to 35 feet long, about 12 to 15 feet at its thickest part, then it tapered off in the front to a teardrop shape." It sat a foot or so off the floor, supported by a wooden cradle. The craft had a slight bluish tint, and it was tremendously shiny.

He walked into the office and delivered the message. "There were several people in there. Nobody was talking, nobody was doing anything; everybody was watching me. They seemed nervous."

He got the signature and was escorted out, after being told to tell no one about what he had seen.

It may have been a very odd way of testing the young officer's integrity. If so, he failed. He spilled the story to a number of UFO researchers. He believed that what he saw was a UFO shot down by a destroyer in the Pacific; he heard rumors about such an incident when he was stationed in San Diego two months later.

Personally, I think it's rather odd for the Navy to transport a UFO all the way to Chicago from the Pacific, when there are UFOs just as good that have crashed nearby. In Milwaukee, for example.

From a formerly classified FBI memo, released through the Freedom of Information Act:

"At 12:07 a.m., 8/27/74, Security Patrol Clerk [name deleted], Intelligence Division, received a call via Command Center telephone from a Major [name deleted], National Military Command Center. Major asked for any information the FBI might have concerning a report that an unidentified object which fell from the sky at Milwaukee, Wisconsin, had been recovered by local police and turned over to the Milwaukee Office of the FBI.

"No information at Intelligence Division, Night Duty Supervisor [name deleted], called Security Patrol Clerk [name deleted], Milwaukee Office, who advised an unidentified object had been recovered by [name deleted]. He said a [name deleted] had called the Milwaukee FBI office to report the recovery. Very little was known about the object, which was described as about 13x8x5 inches, metallic in substance and color, jagged on one side and had an 'internal heat source.' [Name deleted] notified military locally."

I have no idea what the above refers to, or of any sighting made in Milwaukee around that time. But this is a real FBI document. Still, we do not have to make do with just a 13x8x5 part of a UFO when we can get hold of the whole thing.

The night of Jan. 27, 1969, at 12:30 a.m., a UFO was seen to strike the ground six miles east of Hudson, Wis. Two flashes, like lightning, were seen immediately afterward. Police in Prescott, New Richmond and Elmwood all received reports of the incident. It wasn't until the next afternoon that 20 snowmobilers, members of the Snow Trails Unlimited club, assisted by at least one plane, combed a 10-square-mile area, looking for the wreckage. But nothing—no downed aircraft, meteor or UFO—was found.

I prefer to believe that this UFO was plenty good enough for the Navy in Chicago, without their chasing after fashionable West Coast flying saucers. Still, the ways of the Navy are mysterious, indeed. Take for example the next case:

On June 23, 1950, at 11:37 p.m., Northwest flight 2501 was 3,500 feet above sea level, over Battle Creek, Mich. It was 37 minutes from Milwaukee. At that moment, Capt. Robert C. Lind broadcast a typical position report. Everything was fine. On board were 55 passengers, including a General Mills vice president, an AT&T vice president and his family, and a priest.

Roughly an hour and a half later, two Whitefish Bay police officers looked out over Lake Michigan and saw a red light. They watched it for about 10 minutes. They were used to night patrol, but they had never seen anything like it before. It was so odd that they called the Coast Guard.

The Coast Guard Milwaukee Station sent a ship out into the lake. They did not see any strange lights, but they did find a U.S. Navy vessel. The Coast Guard captain asked the Navy captain if he'd seen anything. "No." What were they doing out so late? "Maneuvers."

According to the June 25, 1950, *Chicago Tribune*, the naval vessel had not seen Northwest flight 2501. As a matter of fact, no one has ever seen Northwest flight 2501. It disappeared, 37 minutes from Milwaukee. The Coast Guard didn't know that until the next morning. They launched a search at dawn. Eventually, even the Navy was called in, and they used secret radar and sonar devices to look for the underwater wreckage.

It was never found. No bodies were ever found. No clothing, flotation devices, luggage, not so much as an oil slick.

The flight would have passed directly over the Navy ship and its tight-lipped captain out on "maneuvers."

It took a year, but the Civilian Aeronautics Board finally delivered its findings: "The Board determines that there is not sufficient evidence upon which to make a determination of probable cause. ... None of the radio communications received from the flight, including the last, contained any mention of trouble." The possibility "that this accident resulted from some mechanical failure seems to be remote."

Was the UFO directly responsible, as in the Kinross case? As in the burned-out points in George Wheeler's squad car, in Elmwood?

And what about Elmwood?

In February 1987, U.S. Army Col. Harold E. Phillips, of the Defense Intelligence Agency (the Pentagon's own version of the CIA) convened an interagency group, called the UFO Working Group, to study UFOs on an ongoing basis. At least initially, it included one Army and three Air Force generals, Defense Intelligence Agency scientists, an Army colonel, three officials from the National Security Agency, a supervisor from the CIA's domestic intelligence division and a technical team from the CIA's Science and Technology Directorate.

The group's work, and even its existence, was secret. It was, however, known to former *New York Times* reporter and Pulitzer Prize nominee Howard Blum. While researching a book on the Walker spy family, he was led to the UFO Working Group by a National Security Agency official. Blum developed at least two sources who were members of the group, and he traced its nationwide investigations. He published his findings in the book, *Out There*.

Blum confirmed each detail of the unfolding story of the UFO Working Group with his two sources and, when possible, with others. (Those sources did not include Col. Phillips, the group's convener, however. During a phone conversation from the offices of the Defense Intelligence Agency in the Pentagon, Col. Phillips told Blum that he had never heard of the UFO Working Group. To make matters more suspect, subsequent phone calls to the DIA elicited the response, "We have no record of a Col. Harold Phillips.")

The UFO Working Group's mission was simple: to search for proof of extraterrestrial beings.

In the summer of 1988, after considering many geographic areas with an unusually high number of sightings, the UFO Working Group decided that Elmwood was the "perfect candidate" for study. An investigative team was drawn from the CIA Domestic Collection Division and sent to Elmwood. The intelligence agency, previously forbidden to engage in domestic activities, had in 1981 been cleared by President Reagan to conduct special activities at home, so long as there were no efforts to influence U.S. politics, media or public opinion.

The two men traveled to Elmwood, pretending to be NASA engineers. They interviewed those who had seen UFOs. Alleged landing sites were visited, and soil and geological analyses were conducted. Stories were cross-checked with military records of UFOs. Eyewitnesses' medical records were also studied.

After such a thorough investigation, the team's findings were anticlimactic. Blum's sources reported that, after considering all the many possible explanations for the alleged sightings, it concluded, "We just don't know what's in the skies over Elmwood."

That the Elmwood investigation actually occurred seems to be beyond question. Area newspapers referred with local pride to the visiting "scientists" and their interest.

What may be garbled confirmation comes, again, from UFO researcher Timothy Good. His sources confirm the existence of a Project Aquarius, whose purpose was—or is—to give UFO information to a higher authority. According to Good, a Col. R. "Donny" Phillips "perhaps" led a group within the Defense Intelligence Agency known as a "working committee," which was reorganized in 1986. Aquarius may have been the UFO Working Group.

It gets more complicated. There is a shadowy Las Vegas businessman with alleged Mafia and CIA connections named Robert Bigelow. He has a long-standing interest in UFO research, and in 1995 alone he is said to have donated $1 million to the three largest, private, currently operating UFO investigative groups, the Mutual UFO Network (MUFON), the Fund for UFO Research, and the Center for UFO Study (CUFOS).

The chain of evidence for the existence of the Working Group is now taken up by Philip Klass. Klass is, without a doubt, the top UFO debunker in the country, if not the world. He is not a man to be easily taken in. According to Klass, Bigelow withdrew funding in 1995 after discussing the matter with a Col. John Alexander. Who is Alexander?

According to UFO researcher Michael Corbin, Alexander is Phillips, the head of the UFO Working Group that instigated the Elmwood investigation. Alexander also is the former head of the Los Alamos Nonlethal Weapons research program. Alexander himself has confirmed his Los Alamos work but not his identity as Phillips. Alexander denies that he urged Bigelow to stop the cash flow.

Alexander, who has since retired to Las Vegas, continues to perform nonlethal weapons research for NATO. He is also rumored to be head of the National Institute of Discovery Science in Las Vegas, although he denies that too. The institute is said to be involved in ESP research and theoretical UFO engineering. It describes itself as "a newly formed, privately funded research organization. It focuses on scientific exploration that emphasizes emerging, novel, and sometimes unconventional observations and theories. In its programs, NIDS rigorously employs accepted scientific methods and maintains the highest ethical and quality standards. Because NIDS is a new institution, it is too soon to determine exactly what specific projects will be undertaken. However, the Institute is concentrating on exploring fundamental research on issues concerning the nature and evolution of life and consciousness in the universe, and their modes of interaction."

As it happens, the institute is funded by Robert Bigelow, the previously generous supporter of civilian UFO groups.

Col. Alexander/Phillips was also a member of a group known as the "Aviary," an independent public/private UFO project whose purpose seems to have been the careful release of disinformation in the 1980s to UFO researchers: psychological warfare. The main target was a man named William Moore.

In 1984, William Moore, with Jaime Shandera, posited the existence of a secret governmental UFO study group called Majestic-12, also referred to MJ-12 or MAGIC or MAJICK or Magi. It supposedly was launched in 1947 after the recovery of a crashed flying saucer in Roswell, N.M. It operated out of the brand-new CIA and was answerable only to President Harry Truman. Some argue that, after Eisenhower, no president has even been made aware of the group's existence.

The only evidence supporting the existence of MJ-12 is in the form of a few top-secret government documents that were given by mysterious government figures to William Moore. The existence of Majestic-12 is doubted by most serious UFO researchers, though some ufologists—myself included—believe that there is at least some truth in them. What we may have is a mix of the fantastic and real, bundled in a common document to dissuade serious study.

Coincidentally, one of the key Majestic-12 documents that has subsequently surfaced was mailed anonymously to UFO researchers, postmarked from the state where so much UFO activity seems to be centered, the state that boasts not one, but two, UFO capitals of the world ... Wisconsin.

I don't know if the documents are real. Maybe George does.

Meanwhile, I hope he continues to appreciate my work. I've dedicated this book to him.

ANGELS
AND ANGEL HAIR

After all stories have been assigned to their file folders, we are still left with odd, inexplicable tales that defy categorization. My favorite involves an angel, but there are others that are as sinister as they are bizarre.

What, for example, are we to make of March 19, 1886—the day that five minutes of darkness descended over Oshkosh and other Wisconsin cities? It was as dark as midnight, reported the *Monthly Weather Review*.

"Cities to the west say the same phenomenon was observed there in advance of its appearance here, showing that the wave of darkness passed from west to east. Nothing could be seen to indicate any air currents overhead." So sudden was the onset of darkness that horses were startled and the population of Oshkosh fled into the streets.

Then there is the report made by Harry Anderson, in the summer of 1919, of 20 small men walking in single file on a county road near Barron, Wis. They were bald and pale, and all wore leather shorts held up by suspenders. They wore no shirts. All were mumbling softly to themselves. They approached and passed Anderson, ignoring him. To paranormal investigator Jerome Clark, writing in his 1993 book, *Unexplained!*, this sounded like the centuries-old Celtic tradition of a leprechaunlike race called the Trooping Fairies—an explanation that raises more questions than it answers.

So many mysteries: There is a phantom dog with glowing eyes, near La Crosse; the east-central portion of the state has an out-of-place black panther; sometime in the summer of 1918, on Cedar Lake near Berlin, Mrs. Gus Henschel said she saw a man and a woman disappear before her eyes.

And in October 1881, it rained cobwebs on Milwaukee.

It may be hard to imagine a city shrouded in long, silken strands, but the event was thoroughly documented.

Throughout history there have been reports from all over the world of strange things falling from clear skies. In 1947, freshwater fish fell on Marksville, La. Mussels reportedly fell on Paderhorn, Germany in 1892. It probably wasn't coincidental that both these strange "falls," as such events are termed, occurred soon after nearby storms. Often rains of frogs, fish and the like have been explained by tornadoes or waterspouts. They sweep up the unusual items and carry them high into the air where they're held in place by powerful air currents, only to be dropped miles from the storm. These events are usually not harmful; remember that the fleeing Israelites were saved from starvation by manna, an indescribable edible that rained from the heavens.

Still, one of the creepiest of these storms must surely be the Milwaukee cobweb shower. In ufology, this material is known as "angel hair," and some suspect that it is ionized air sleeting off an electromagnetic field surrounding a UFO.

Observers said the cobwebs seemed to have descended from a great height over Lake Michigan. Green Bay, Fort Howard and Sheboygan also were struck by the strange shower. In Milwaukee, the strands were described as measuring between 2 feet and several rods, while in Green Bay some webs were as long as 60 feet. They were strong and very white, and fell so thick "as to annoy the eye," according to an 1881 issue of *Scientific American*.

"Curiously, there is no mention, in any of the reports that we have seen, of the presence of spiders in the general shower of webs," the magazine reported.

Where the cobwebs came from, no one was able to explain. However, Charles Darwin, on his famous research voyage aboard the

Beagle, also reported a shower of cobwebs while his ship was 60 miles from land. Similar storms struck Port Hope, Ontario, in 1948, and Montreal in 1962.

Moving from angel's hair to angels, I'll close on a reassuring account of some spook lights that made themselves home in a church.

In July 1970, hundreds of people gathered around St. Mary's Catholic Church in Burlington to watch a strange glow that appeared halfway up the steeple. The witnesses didn't know it then, but the light's appearance may have saved their church.

The glow was first sighted on Sunday, July 12. Some described it as a bright blue light. Others said it was a twinkling light that changed colors. It appeared again the next night near a ball that supported the cross at the top of the steeple, 200 feet in the air.

By Friday night, the intersection of State and McHenry streets in Burlington was jammed with curious spectators. They were disappointed. The light did not appear. Visitors Saturday night were also let down.

Church officials refused to comment on the light, though others offered explanations. A Burlington police officer, who claimed to have seen the light several times in one night, said that it disappeared when the streetlights went off in the morning. He theorized that the glow was a reflection of the lights. Other explanations ranged from swarming fireflies to St. Elmo's fire, a real phenomenon usually observed at sea or on the spires of tall buildings.

On Thursday, July 23, 1970, the light again was spotted. There were around 200 spectators, among them Don Reed, a reporter for the *Racine Journal-Times*.

"The little light, above the lighted clock and the bell tower, was located on the tip of one of the lesser spires in the Gothic-style steeple," he wrote.

"It appeared reddish-orange in color and varied in intensity, at times being barely discernible and at other times being bright. It had the appearance of a small 'twinkle light,' such as used on Christmas trees."

At 10:55 p.m. the light disappeared, glowing white for a second before leaving. The reporter judged that the light could not have been a reflection because the steeple was painted a dull gray. Nor could it have been produced by faulty wiring, as others had suggested, because there was no wiring in the steeple above the circuit that ran to the clock lights.

The steeple was checked, however, and it was discovered that the church's lightning-protection system was not properly attached to the cross on the top of the steeple. This was a potentially dangerous situation as it meant that electricity, after a lightning strike, could arc back to the steeple and start a fire.

Was the strange glow just static electricity? Or was it a dancing angel, warning that the church—only 25 miles from Lake Michigan and its fierce storms—was unprotected?

Whether or not the light was an angel, it acted as one. The system was repaired, the church was made safe, and the light disappeared.

Until we need it again?

PLACE-NAME INDEX

Unless otherwise indicated,
cities and villages named are within Wisconsin.

MORE BOOKS ON WISCONSIN
FROM WISCONSIN TRAILS

Great Wisconsin Taverns   *Dennis Boyer*

Great Wisconsin Restaurants   *Dennis Getto*

Foods That Made Wisconsin Famous   *Richard J. Baumann*

Great Minnesota Walks: 49 Strolls, Rambles, Hikes, and Treks
Wm. Chad McGrath

Creating a Perennial Garden in the Midwest   *Joan Severa*

The Spirit of Door County: A Photographic Essay   *Darryl R. Beers*

Up North Wisconsin: A Region for All Seasons   *Sharyn Alden*

The M-Files: True Reports of Minnesota's Unexplained Phenomena   *Jay Rath*

The I-Files: True Reports of Unexplained Phenomena in Illinois   *Jay Rath*

Great Wisconsin Walks: 45 Strolls, Rambles, Hikes, and Treks
Wm. Chad McGrath

Great Weekend Adventures   *the Editors of Wisconsin Trails*

Best Canoe Trails of Southern Wisconsin   *Michael E. Duncanson*

County Parks of Wisconsin: 600 Parks You Can Visit Featuring 25 Favorites
Jeannette and Chet Bell

The Wisconsin Traveler's Companion: A Guide to Country Sights
Jerry Apps and Julie Sutter-Blair

W Is for Wisconsin   *Dori Hillestad Butler and Eileen Dawson*

Walking Tours of Wisconsin's Historic Towns
Lucy Rhodes, Elizabeth McBride, and Anita Matcha

Wisconsin: The Story of the Badger State   *Norman K. Risjord*

Paddling Northern Wisconsin   *Mike Svob*

Best Wisconsin Bike Trips   *Phil Van Valkenberg*

Barns of Wisconsin   *Jerry Apps*

Portrait of the Past: A Photographic Journey Through Wisconsin 1865-1920
Howard Mead, Jill Dean, and Susan Smith

Trails Media Group, Inc.
P.O. Box 5650, Madison, WI 53705
(800) 236-8088
e-mail: info@wistrails.com
www.trailsbooks.com